BALZAC'S LOVE LETTERS
CORRESPONDENCE AND THE LITERARY IMAGINATION

LEGENDA

LEGENDA is the Modern Humanities Research Association's book imprint for new research in the Humanities. Founded in 1995 by Malcolm Bowie and others within the University of Oxford, Legenda has always been a collaborative publishing enterprise, directly governed by scholars. The Modern Humanities Research Association (MHRA) joined this collaboration in 1998, became half-owner in 2004, in partnership with Maney Publishing and then Routledge, and has since 2016 been sole owner. Titles range from medieval texts to contemporary cinema and form a widely comparative view of the modern humanities, including works on Arabic, Catalan, English, French, German, Greek, Italian, Portuguese, Russian, Spanish, and Yiddish literature. Editorial boards and committees of more than 60 leading academic specialists work in collaboration with bodies such as the Society for French Studies, the British Comparative Literature Association and the Association of Hispanists of Great Britain & Ireland.

The MHRA encourages and promotes advanced study and research in the field of the modern humanities, especially modern European languages and literature, including English, and also cinema. It aims to break down the barriers between scholars working in different disciplines and to maintain the unity of humanistic scholarship. The Association fulfils this purpose through the publication of journals, bibliographies, monographs, critical editions, and the MHRA Style Guide, and by making grants in support of research. Membership is open to all who work in the Humanities, whether independent or in a University post, and the participation of younger colleagues entering the field is especially welcomed.

RESEARCH MONOGRAPHS IN FRENCH STUDIES

The *Research Monographs in French Studies* (RMFS) form a separate series within the Legenda programme and are published in association with the Society for French Studies. Individual members of the Society are entitled to purchase all RMFS titles at a discount.

The series seeks to publish the best new work in all areas of the literature, thought, theory, culture, film and language of the French-speaking world. Its distinctiveness lies in the relative brevity of its publications (50,000–60,000 words). As innovation is a priority of the series, volumes should predominantly consist of new material, although, subject to appropriate modification, previously published research may form up to one third of the whole. Proposals may include critical editions as well as critical studies. They should be sent with one or two sample chapters for consideration to Professor Diana Knight, Department of French and Francophone Studies, University of Nottingham, University Park, Nottingham NG7 2RD.

❖

Editorial Committee
Diana Knight, University of Nottingham (General Editor)
Bill Burgwinkle, King's College, Cambridge
Janice Carruthers, Queen's University Belfast
Shirley Jordan, Queen Mary, University of London
Neil Kenny, All Souls College, Oxford
Jennifer Yee, Christ Church, Oxford

Advisory Committee
Wendy Ayres-Bennett, Murray Edwards College, Cambridge
Celia Britton, University College London
Ann Jefferson, New College, Oxford
Sarah Kay, New York University
Michael Moriarty, University of Cambridge
Keith Reader, University of Glasgow

PUBLISHED IN THIS SERIES

www.legendabooks.com

Balzac's Love Letters

Correspondence and the Literary Imagination

❖

Ewa Szypula

l

LEGENDA

Research Monographs in French Studies 52
Modern Humanities Research Association
2016

Published by Legenda
An imprint of the Modern Humanities Research Association
Salisbury House, Station Road, Cambridge CB1 2LA

ISBN 978-1-910887-18-9 (HB)
ISBN 978-1-78188-345-7 (PB)

First published 2016

Copy-Editor: Charlotte Brown

CONTENTS

❖

For R. A. Bates and for W. A. Szypula
— with love and gratitude

ACKNOWLEDGEMENTS

❖

This project would not have been possible without the help and support of many people. I would like to offer my special thanks to the following:

My supervisors at King's College London, Anne Green and Siobhan McIlvanney, who devoted hours of their time to reading and discussing my original PhD thesis.

Tim Farrant and Damien Catani, my examiners, who took the time to read and comment on my finished thesis in depth, and suggested many new possible avenues of further research.

My MA supervisor, Diana Knight, for her insights, advice, and astounding knowledge of Balzac, and for her support during my studies at the University of Nottingham.

Rosemary Chapman, for her generous support, advice, and positivity during the writing of the book manuscript.

Francesco Manzini, for proof-reading the final manuscript and for his unflagging encouragement throughout.

I should also like to thank the anonymous readers of the initial manuscript, whose insightful feedback contributed enormously to the quality of the final draft.

I gratefully acknowledge the support of the Modern Humanities Research Association, and the Department of French and Francophone Studies at the University of Nottingham, who provided the funding for this project.

My friends Anneke Ely, Estelle Murail, Pippa Rimmer, Hannah Morcos, Lucy Marx, Anna Orhanen, Katharine Thorne, Céline Candiard, Alex Mével, Vanessa Pansi, Yvonne Choinowski, Maureen and Peter Bates, and Emma Britton — you light up my world with your kindness and generosity.

Ania, Kasia, and mama — for all the different ways you've supported me and helped me become an amazing grown-up writer.

And Richard — you get your thank you in another form: maybe on a Post-it note, or in a poem, or in a love letter.

'Sous ces phrases insensibles et sottes peut-être, il y aura
mille pensées pour vous.'

[Underneath these cold and perhaps ridiculous sentences,
there will be a thousand thoughts for you.]

Honoré de Balzac to Éveline Hanska, January 1833

AUTHOR'S NOTE

❖

The following abbreviations have been used throughout:

CH   Honoré de Balzac, *La Comédie humaine*, ed. by Pierre-Georges Castex, 12 vols (Paris: Gallimard, Bibliotheque de la Pléiade, 1976–81)

Corr   Honoré de Balzac, *Correspondance*, ed. by Roger Pierrot and Hervé Yon, 2 vols (Paris: Gallimard, 2006–11)

LMH   Honoré de Balzac, *Lettres à Madame Hanska*, ed. by Roger Pierrot, 2 vols (Paris: Laffont, Bouquins, 1990)

PR   Honoré de Balzac, *Premiers romans*, ed. by André Lorant, 2 vol (Paris: Laffont, Bouquins, 1999)

On Madame Hanska's name: Madame Hanska is variously referred to by critics as Ève, Éva, Évelina, or Éveline. It seems that she introduced herself to Balzac as Évelina — a name which Balzac then inserts into his novel *Le Médecin de campagne* (1833), and which, as we shall see, he playfully amends throughout the correspondence (derivations include Ève, Évelette, Line, and even a masculinized version, 'mon Évelin').

Born on 24 December, which in the Polish calendar is the name day of Adam and Eve, Ewelina Rzewuska (to use the Polish spelling) was christened after the biblical first woman, in accordance with the old custom of naming children after the saint on whose nameday they were born. Her birth certificate is missing and therefore it is not clear whether her full name was in fact Ewelina or Ewa — the two often being considered as versions of the same name.

Where I have chosen to refer to Hanska by her first name, the name Éveline is used (except when an explicit reference is being made to Balzac's other names for her); this is done to avoid confusion with the fictional Évelina of *Le Médecin de campagne*.

PREFACE

❖

The correspondence of Honoré de Balzac and his literary lover Éveline Hanska began when she sent him an anonymous letter (dated 28 February 1832) to tell him of her reaction to his latest novel, *La Peau de chagrin*.

While it praised his *Scènes de la vie privée*, her letter condemned the more negative portrayal of women in *La Peau de chagrin*, urging Balzac to return to his earlier, more sensitive depictions of female characters. 'En lisant vos ouvrages mon cœur a tressailli; vous élevez la femme à sa juste dignité; l'amour chez elle est une vertu céleste, une émanation divine; j'admire en vous cette admirable sensibilité d'âme qui vous l'a fait deviner' [Whilst reading your works, my heart skipped a beat; you raise women to their rightful level of dignity; love for them is a celestial virtue, a divine emanation; I admire this admirable sensitivity of your soul which made you perceive this], Éveline Hanska wrote in a subsequent letter, on 7 November 1832.[1]

It is curious that it should have been this particular novel which brought the two correspondents together; for of course *La Peau de chagrin* depicts, amongst other things, a young writer's quest for an unattainable, exotic, foreign (Russian) woman. That a letter bearing a Russian postmark should then land on Balzac's desk, coming, in all likelihood, from a 'princesse russe ou polonaise' [Russian or Polish princess],[2] must have seemed to Balzac to be an odd happenstance; it would in fact be the first in a string of coincidences linking the plot of *La Peau de chagrin* to this most bizarre and enduring of love affairs. The story of Balzac and his Eve is no less strange than are the love stories depicted in this novel. That Balzac should marry his 'princess' just months before he died, at a point where his life force was already almost spent, is another cruel and unintended parallel with the fictional story.

This study does not seek to engage in a detailed comparison of Balzac's correspondence with the text of *La Peau de chagrin*. However, the many parallels between the correspondence and this novel in particular point towards some important notions found in Balzac's writing. As will be seen, both Balzac's fiction and his letter-writing are discernibly marked by the Romantic predilection for the imagined as opposed to the real — a concept which is so crucial to the closing pages of *La Peau de chagrin*. We also realise, upon comparing the two, the extent to which Balzac's fiction and his letters seep into one another, in often surprising ways.

The letters *are* a sort of fiction, Madame Hanska writing to someone she knew and admired as an author, and Balzac using them as an exercise in self-valorization and self-creation. A detailed study of Balzac's letters to Hanska seems to invite the reader to go back to the text of *La Peau de chagrin*, and go searching for familiar echoes. The quotations I have placed at the beginning of each chapter are, I hope, just such an invitation.

Notes to the Preface

1. Honoré de Balzac, *Lettres à Madame Hanska*, ed. by Roger Pierrot, 2 vols (Paris: Laffont, Bouquins, 1990) (hereafter *LMH*), I, 14 (7 November 1832). All translations into English are my own; for their helpful suggestions, I am very grateful to Estelle Murail and Alex Mével.

2. See *LMH*, I, 13.

INTRODUCTION

❖

Comme tous les grands enfants, j'aspirai secrètement à de belles amours.
[Like all children at heart, I secretly yearned for beautiful passions.]
BALZAC, *La Peau de chagrin* (*CH*, x, 128)

In 1832, Balzac received an anonymous fan letter, bearing a Russian postmark and a foreign coat of arms, from a woman who signed her name simply 'L'Étrangère' (meaning 'The Stranger', or 'Foreign Woman'). What followed was a long correspondence with the *Étrangère*, Éveline Hanska, which lasted sixteen years, and which resulted in their marriage not months before Balzac died.

Balzac was no stranger to receiving anonymous fan mail from women. However, this particular correspondence was clearly unique, as it outlasted all others, and led Balzac to pursue this woman until she married him. She herself, it would transpire, was already unhappily married to a much older Polish count, who died in 1841. The correspondence flattered Balzac's vanity; in an early letter, the *Étrangère* told him how much she admired his works, and hinted that she would like to help his genius become 'divin' [divine].[1] The pair went on to meet at Neuchâtel, in Switzerland, in September 1833, where a kiss was stolen and a promise of marriage made.[2] A sexual relationship was probably cemented on their next meeting, a few months later in Geneva — the letters, which mention a 'jour inoubliable' [unforgettable day], are reticent as to the details.[3] Yet the promised marriage did not take place until 1850. In the meantime, Balzac wrote her a lot of letters.

The intriguing figure of Éveline Hanska has since been the focus of several biographical studies. Her influence on Balzac's work, her family life, the social circles within which she moved, and her personal diary have all attracted critical attention.[4] To date, however, there has been no in-depth, extensive critical study of the Balzac-Hanska letters. Initially published between 1899–1950 under the title of *Lettres à l'Étrangère*, the letters were reprinted in two volumes in 1990, under the title *Lettres à Madame Hanska*. The correspondence has a special place among Balzac's writings, and has even been treated as a distinct corpus by publishers, perhaps for purely logistical reasons: given the sheer volume of the letters in question, incorporating them into his general *Correspondance* would be difficult.

Balzac wrote to her about anything and everything — his daily struggles with work and money, his family, his thoughts and dreams — with his letters often (very self-consciously) resembling a journal rather than a correspondence. Flaubert later implied that he considered Balzac's general correspondence to be boring, precisely because of the prosaic nature of some of the concerns recorded in it: 'Balzac ne s'inquiète ni de l'Art, ni de la religion, ni de l'humanité, ni de la science. Lui et toujours lui, ses dettes, ses meubles, son imprimerie! [...] Quelle vie lamentable!' [Balzac does not preoccupy himself with Art, nor with religion, nor with humanity, nor science. Him and always him, his debts, his furnishings, his printing business! [...] What a pathetic life!].[5] Flaubert's claim, however, is less applicable to the letters to Hanska. Aside from their many comments on visual art, sculpture, and music, Balzac's letters to her also dwell at length on the creative life of the artist: the difficult and the happy times, the all-absorbing toils, the delight in one's creative faculties, the jubilation at completing a work.[6] That the letters also record Balzac's most trivial thoughts and comments is not surprising, given that this was a correspondence in which the pair frequently did not see one another for up to eight years at a time, meaning that letters were their chief means of contact. It is thanks to the distance between the two — she lived in Russian-occupied Poland, he in France — that we are now privy to this valuable document in which every major aspect of Balzac's life, from his creative processes to his everyday concerns, is described. The Balzac-Hanska correspondence has been useful to Balzac's biographers and critics, for it gives not only details of his life but also those relating to the genesis and redrafting of his literary output.

As with any correspondence, Balzac's love letters must be treated cautiously if used as a biographical source, and the views expressed therein cannot necessarily be taken at face value. As we shall see in Chapter 1, Balzac's correspondence contains numerous exaggerations and some downright lies. When Roger Pierrot suggests, then, that in Balzac's letters 'nous avons la création spontanée d'un écrivain qui se surveille peu' [we have the spontaneous creation of a writer who rarely watches himself], we must be wary.[7] Although Balzac may sometimes claim that his letters are spontaneous and never overworked,[8] not only are there other times when he completely contradicts this,[9] but also, as Ruth Amossy points out, the very fact of writing to another person, whose judgment and personality one must take into account, means that the letters end up 'censored' from the outset; to paraphrase Catherine Kerbat-Orecchioni, 'le "tu" exerce un contrôle permanent sur le discours du "je"' [the 'you' permanently controls the discourse of the 'I'].[10]

Balzac himself suggests that a correspondence does not necessarily give a clear picture of the person behind the letter. Writing to a woman named 'Louise', with whom he entered into a brief epistolary relationship from 1836 to 1837, Balzac remarks:

> Ainsi, que saurez-vous de moi? presque rien, car, pour me connaître, il faut me pratiquer, et longtemps. Que puis-je savoir de vous par des lettres, quelque confiantes qu'elles soient? Peuvent-elles dire ces petits faits de tous les jours, de tous les moments, qui sont la vie.[11]

> [So, what will you actually know about me? Almost nothing, for to know me you need to learn to get to know me, and this must be done over a long period of time. What can I know of you through your letters, however revealing they may be? Can they tell me those little everyday things, those everyday moments, which are your life.]

This point is underscored in *Modeste Mignon* (1844): 'les lettres que nous écrivions seraient l'expression du moment où elles nous échapperaient, et non pas le sens général de nos caractères' [the letters we write are the expression of the moment in which they have escaped us, and not the general meaning of our characters].[12]

This monograph proposes a reappraisal of the letters with a focus on critical analysis, approaching the letters as text. As scholars have suggested, a writer's correspondence, which proceeds 'de la même plume' [from the same pen] as his fiction, can therefore be seen as being more fictional than that of anyone else; with regards to Balzac's letters, I would suggest that it is more fruitful, therefore, to treat their content as 'writing' rather than as face-value statements.[13] The status of Balzac's letters to Madame Hanska as a 'love correspondence' has perhaps also led to certain assumptions being made about them, based on our preconceptions of this genre. Ruth Amossy suggests that the love letter places communication and interaction above anything else.[14] Yet the love letter can, especially perhaps if its author is a writer of fiction by trade, hide ulterior motives, and, as Vincent Kaufmann demonstrates in his study on writers' correspondence, does not necessarily have communication as its goal.[15] The line between the fictional and the real can become blurred. The love letter of a writer is in fact situated somewhere between reality and fiction, veering from the real towards the fictional (as Anne-Marie Baron points out, Balzac's correspondence may to an extent be seen as a construction of his own 'roman personnel', or personal novel).[16]

Certainly, Balzac's letters are not a 'novel', in the literary sense of the term, as they have sometimes been labelled by critics; indeed, this monograph seeks to dispel this and other *idées reçues*, which have been unwittingly propagated by critical studies. As Kaufmann points out, the long correspondence of writers rarely makes for scintillating reading — and is best read lying down.[17] Balzac himself expresses concerns that Hanska may be getting bored of his endless letters and their repetitions: '*Cara*, vous finirez par [...] vous ennuyer de mes jérémiades' [*Cara*, you will end up [...] getting bored of my jeremiads].[18]

Yet although he does not always consider them to be exciting reading for Madame Hanska, Balzac in fact regards his own letters very highly. For example, on 15 November 1838, he describes his despair after he mislaid a letter he wrote to Hanska and spent three hours searching fruitlessly for it; he writes 'je la pleure, car pour moi toute expression d'âme tombée dans le gouffre de l'oubli me semble irréparable' [I am mourning this letter, for to me any expression of the soul which falls into the abyss of oblivion is an irreparable loss].[19] Crucially, we note that he is upset over the loss of his own letter, not one of hers; while to Louise he had claimed that a letter of his can reveal almost nothing of value to her, and in *Modeste Mignon* he later suggests that letters are simply the impulse of a moment, *his* own letter is much more highly prized. We can infer from this that what is most valuable about the relationship with Madame Hanska is not necessarily what she herself might say or do, but rather the change she might bring about in him as a person and the things he ends up doing — the writing he ends up producing — as a result.

The importance which Balzac accords to letter-writing is reiterated in *Le Médecin de campagne* (which, as I shall discuss in Chapter 1, owes much of the inspiration for its love story to the earliest days of the Hanska correspondence). The protagonist Benassis describes three letters exchanged with Évelina, two of which remain in his possession, and which form the sum total of mementoes left from their love affair. Interestingly, it is of *his* letter to her (of which he has kept a draft) that Benassis feels most protective: '[ce brouillon] représente aujourd'hui toutes mes joies, mais flétries' [[this draft] today represents all my joys, withered though they be] (*CH*, IX, 568).

This crucial insight into Balzac's treatment of his own letters — the writerly enjoyment of his own words, the significance accorded to the expression of his thoughts — expressed here at the climactic moment of the love story in *Le Médecin*, has so far escaped the notice of Balzac scholars. The letter-writer's reluctance to dispose of his own writing suggests that his letters have their own distinct value: they are self-conscious constructs, and each is not only a 'commentaire sur le grand homme littéraire qu'il [Balzac] veut devenir' [comment on the great literary figure that he [Balzac] wants to become] and an opportunity to record his 'activité imaginaire' [imaginary activity], but is also in itself an exercise in the novelist's creative imagination, a welcome opportunity to observe the effects of his correspondence on himself.[20] That this special significance of the letter to its writer should find its way into *Le Médecin* (a story composed specially for Éveline Hanska), reinforces not only the special status of the writer's letter, but also points to the slippage between the genres of fiction and correspondence.

One of the aims of this monograph is to look at precisely this kind of overlap between the writing of letters and of novels; throughout this study I shall be examining this interrelationship between the two in more detail. The letters have for the most part been seen as source material for biographical and critical studies of Balzac, and have been seen as a source of understanding for Balzac's novels, a 'paratext' or a 'literary metalanguage' to his fiction.[21] My study takes a different approach, showing how the novels feed into the letters, and how they can in some cases themselves be said to form a part of the correspondence. In this monograph, the letters emerge as a prima facie example of Balzac's fictional imagination. We can in fact read Balzac's novels as constituting 'additional material' to the letters. Of *Pierrette* (1840), for instance, Balzac wrote to Madame Hanska, 'Vous trouverez ici mille choses que j'ai à vous dire et que le papier ne me permet plus d'exprimer' [You will find in here a thousand things which I want to say, but which the paper no longer allows me to express].[22] We can read this in at least two ways. One is that, his page having come to an end, Balzac suggests that Hanska can begin reading *Pierrette* and thereby continue her conversation with him. Or we can read this to mean that letters can only express so much, and novels can be made to contain supplementary material, or thoughts which one cannot or prefers not to spell out in a letter (for revealing something of one's innermost convictions is sometimes better done in a veiled way, by allegory, rather than by saying it clearly and so risking criticism and rejection).[23] As editors of *La Comédie humaine* have noted, Balzac writes versions of Éveline into novels such as *Le Médecin de campagne*, *Séraphîta* (1835), and *Albert Savarus* (1842), variously hoping to instruct, persuade, or seduce her, or using the novels to plead his cause. By placing the primary emphasis on the letters to Madame Hanska, I show how the novels can be read as further missives to Éveline, continuations of the correspondence.

Critics have linked Balzac's rapid physical decline to his unhappy and fruitless chase after Madame Hanska; following her around the various cities of Europe rather than remaining productive, Balzac is said to have exhausted his physical resources.[24] Éveline has been portrayed as having forced upon Balzac all the physical suffering of his later years, and as being the cause of his creative impotence towards the end of his life.[25] The negative view of Madame Hanska, which seems to have originated in the calumny of her by her contemporaries after Balzac's death (for example, she was famously accused of 'consoling' herself with a lover as Balzac lay on his death bed) seems to persist even in recent critical studies of the letters.[26] Scholars have occasionally interpreted key extracts from Balzac's letters in the light of earlier negative portrayals of Madame Hanska, and these now merit a reappraisal. Anne McCall Saint-Saëns, for instance, sees the letters to Madame Hanska as 'un cas exemplaire d'impuissance épistolaire' [a prime example of epistolary impotence] on Balzac's part.[27] This analysis, however, is based on the assumption that Balzac's 'epistolary project' has, as its goal, to 'faire écrire la femme' [make the woman write] (Ibid., p. 47). I would argue that Balzac's letters seek instead to '[d]écrire la femme' [write, or describe, the woman] — imagining her, creating her, writing her past and her future — for his own ends.

As we shall see in Chapters 1 and 2, Balzac does not necessarily seek to find out anything about the mysterious Étrangère, contrary perhaps to the suggestion made by Uwe Vogel that Balzac was keen to learn the identities of his anonymous correspondents.[28] 'Avoir de l'amour toutes les poésies sans voir l'amant! quelle suave débauche!' [To have all the poetry of love and not see the lover! What suave debauchery!], wrote Balzac in Modeste Mignon, suggesting that to have only limited knowledge of one's correspondent can in fact enhance one's experience of the relationship (CH, I, 510). While Balzac did want to know certain details, such as the Étrangère's full name, he would use these details to his own ends, continuing to create his own version of her. Through this correspondence, Balzac not only reinforces his own position as creator and author, but is also modelling himself on her letters, and taking her responses as a cue to the next 'role' he will assume. The way the letters allow Balzac to play with multiple identities is something I shall explore in Chapter 2. Balzac willingly exploits the epistolary dialogue, with a great deal of writerly enjoyment, welcoming the purported shortcomings of the medium (the distance, the separation, the lack of the Other's presence) and uses this wonderfully imperfect space as a blank screen of representation onto which to project his 'brouillons de soi' [drafts of the self].[29]

Balzac described correspondence as a Proteus, or shape-shifter, in his essay 'De la correspondance' [On Correspondence] in the Physiologie du mariage (1829) (CH, XI, 1095). He was referring to the fact that a 'correspondence' can take many forms: a love letter can be written on the cover of a book; a flower worn in a certain way at a ball can send a message which also belongs to the realm of 'correspondence'. The correspondence with Éveline Hanska, which initially took the form of newspaper announcements (not knowing her address, Balzac replied to the Étrangère by placing an advertisement in the Gazette de France), continued to change shape.[30] It took the form not only of letters (private love letters supplemented by 'dummy' ones, lettres ostensibles, which could be shown to Éveline's family), but also of dedications in novels, and, as the example of *Pierrette* suggests, even of the text of actual novels themselves. When Balzac begs Madame Hanska for a piece of grey silk from her dress for the binding of the manuscript of *Séraphîta*, this symbolic enrobing of the *œuvre* in a piece of Éveline's 'drap furtif, [...] vêtement silencieux' [furtive fabric, [...] silent cloth] illustrates very aptly the kind of interrelationship between objects, works and letters which Balzac apparently had in mind when writing 'De la correspondance'.[31]

Balzac's comment on the Protean nature of correspondence has been interpreted in another way by Brigitte Diaz, who suggests that 'les correspondances sont des Protées parce qu'au cours de leur existence, souvent longue, elles connaissent plusieurs vies' [correspondences are Protean because over the course of their often lengthy existence they go through several lives].[32] The long correspondence of writers undergoes many shifts in tone over time. This is the case with Balzac's letters: the earliest letters (dating from 1832–33) have a crafted, literary quality, with Balzac trying to showcase his literary talents; as he and Éveline begin to fall in love (a process leading to, and cemented by, their first meeting at Neuchâtel in 1833), the letters gain in intensity; they become passionate, exalted outpourings of sentiment, with words tumbling over each other in the writer's haste to set them down on paper.[33] However, once this honeymoon period eventually ends, the exalted, informal 'tu' of the lovers reverts to a somewhat embarrassed and more cautious 'vous'. As Kaufmann suggests, a letter-writer is commonly forced to seek out stronger words to 'top' the ones he has previously used, and this process of raising the stakes cannot continue indefinitely.[34] We might here apply a suggestion by Owen Heathcote, who proposes that Balzac's letters to Madame Hanska 'finissent, justement, par s'user à force de vacuité ou d'emphase' [end up wearing themselves out, through sheer vacuity or grandiloquence].[35] Yet the Balzac-Hanska correspondence, though it does vary in intensity and intimacy, does not completely 'dry up'.

Another interpretation of Balzac's vision of the correspondence as a 'shape-shifter', which his other writings support, is the idea that a correspondence is read and reinterpreted differently by different readers. Balzac's suggestion in *Le Père Goriot* (1834–35) that 'une lettre est une âme' [a letter is a soul] to someone with an emotional investment in their correspondent's words, is essentially a comment on the subjectivity of reading.[36] My study therefore culminates in a discussion of the twin motifs of reading and rereading in the letters to Madame Hanska, exploring Balzac's portrayal of himself as a (re)reader. My analysis is partly inspired by the work of Roland Barthes, whose study of Balzac's *Sarrasine* (1830) in *S/Z* pinpoints precisely the significance of rereading, and the role of the (re)reader as producer of a text.[37] This is an idea which Balzac had himself proposed in the *Physiologie du mariage* when he wrote that 'Lire, c'est créer peut-être à deux' [Reading is creating, perhaps together], explaining how a reader appropriates the writer's words and makes them his or her own.[38] As Barthes suggests, Balzac's apparently 'readerly' (*lisible*) texts in fact lend themselves to the continuous possibility of rereading and critical reappraisal. In Balzac's letters, Balzac himself emerges as a rereader, showing how subsequent rereadings can continue to 'haunt' the text of a letter long after it has been considered finished and consigned to the past.[39]

By writing letters, and through his rereadings of Éveline's letters (thereby returning to past events), Balzac seems to be seeking a kind of therapy, an assimilation or processing of their contents, an act we may compare to Freud's *Durcharbeiten*, or 'working through'; he constructs and reworks narratives around his correspondent's letters which allow him to make sense of their (occasionally troubling) contents. This process, I will show, is directly related to Balzac's method of literary creation, which depends on the collection and reinterpretation of real and psychical objects. Collection, rereading and reinterpretation beget creation, and Balzac's relationship to Éveline's letters-as-objects is central to this process.

Today, only three of her letters to Balzac remain; two of these are written in calligraphy (not in her handwriting and therefore untraceable to her); another is a humorous note with a joke signature.[40] A key hurdle in analyzing Balzac's correspondence with Madame Hanska is the fact that that we do not have access to her side of it. Madame Hanska requested that her letters to Balzac be burnt, following an alleged blackmail attempt by Balzac's then-housekeeper, Louise de Brugnol. (Doubts persist as to whether this blackmail attempt really happened, or whether the whole episode was an elaborate lie constructed by Balzac in order to hide the truth about his relationship with de Brugnol).[41] Balzac complied with the request on 3 September 1847, commemorating the sad occasion with true writerly aplomb:

> Voici chère comtesse le plus affreux et le plus triste jour de ma vie, j'ai accompli tout à l'heure le plus grand sacrifice que je pusse faire, je me suis séparé de mon plus cher trésor. Tout est anéanti [...]. Je les ai jetées au feu une à une en regardant les dates! J'ai sauvé quelques fleurs, quelques échantillons de robe, une ceinture; mais ma douleur, je la garde pour moi.[42]

> [Today, dear countess, is the worst and saddest day of my life, I have just accomplished the greatest sacrifice I could possibly do, I have parted with my treasure. It is all gone [...]. I threw them into the fire one by one, looking at the dates! I saved some flowers, a few scraps of your dresses, a belt; but as for my pain, I am keeping it for myself.]

We might console ourselves with the idea — be it only a retrospective illusion — that Madame Hanska's letters are not needed; that we do not have Éveline's side of the correspondence is in a sense no handicap to studying Balzac's letters, for what these paint is first and foremost a picture of a creative writer at work. We get the sense that these letters can exist on their own, as 'monologues'; they do not necessarily require the context of the dialogue with the Other in order to be appreciated in themselves.

In his unfinished essay on the famous Goethe-Bettina correspondence (to which Balzac's letters allude several times, and which profoundly influenced one of his works), Balzac makes the point that if one of the correspondents were to fall silent, writing could go on notwithstanding.[43] Indeed, the figure of the correspondent, be it Balzac or Madame Hanska — or any letter-writer — may well be a mere 'pretext' for writing letters:

> Goethe n'aimait pas Bettina. Mettez à la place de Goethe une grosse pierre, le Sphinx qu'aucune puissance n'a pu dégager de ses sables au désert, et les lettres

de Bettina peuvent avoir lieu très bien. Au rebours de la fable de Pygmalion, plus Bettina écrit, plus Goethe se pétrifie, plus ses lettres deviennent glaciales. [...] Comme elle n'aime point elle-même Goethe, [...] Goethe est un prétexte à lettres, elle continue, elle écrit son journal de petite fille. (*CH*, I, 1335)

[Goethe did not love Bettina. You can put a great big rock in Goethe's place, a Sphinx whom no power could move from the desert sands, and Bettina's letters could still very well exist. In direct contrast to the Pygmalion fable, the more Bettina writes, the more Goethe becomes petrified, the more his letters turn to ice. [...] Since she does not love Goethe at all either, [...] Goethe is a mere pretext for letter-writing, she carries on, writing her little girl's diary.]

This scathing portrayal of her as the author of a 'little girl's diary' is more revealing than Balzac may have intended: in his letters to Madame Hanska, he occasionally takes up just such a role — that of the childish correspondent writing letters to nowhere, and not necessarily paying attention to whether or not his reply is being solicited. There are indeed instances in the correspondence where Balzac is writing letters to Éveline and receiving no reply; the longer she is silent, the more he writes, thus becoming rather like the immature letter-writer he describes in this unfinished essay. Here, Balzac suggests that the correspondents are to a large extent autonomous, talking to themselves, enchanted by the sound of their own voices; the Other is, at best, an excuse to write letters, which serve as a means of conversing with the self.

The structure of this study to a large extent attempts to follow the chronological development of the correspondence, in order to explore Balzac's treatment of it as an opportunity for fictional and literary creation, for role-playing and for developing his literary theories, and to trace their development as it progresses.[44] Thus in Chapter 1, 'The Blank Page and the Palimpsest', we witness the creative processes employed by Balzac at the beginning of the correspondence, in the service of a relationship with a woman he had never met. She is simultaneously represented as a 'blank page' to be filled by Balzac's imagination, and as a palimpsestic overwriting of all the women who came into his life before her. Subsequent chapters show how Balzac's use of literary devices in the correspondence evolved and changed, as Balzac grew bolder in his efforts to retain creative control of the relationship. Chapter 2, 'Performance and Play', shows how the letters allow Balzac to reinvent himself, and aspects of his relationship with his mistress, by 'scripting' a variety of roles for them both to play. The increasingly pronounced focus, in Balzac's letters, on the physical and the sensual informs the writing of Chapter 3, 'Balzac Collector, Rereader, and Storyteller', in which we move to a discussion of letters as fetishized objects, and to Balzac's collecting practices, which in turn inform his practices of storytelling. This chapter explores the gradually emerging figure of Balzac the collector — of letters, of memories, and of stories. The letters function as a 'collection' in several ways: they bring small gifts and tokens of affection from the lover; they serve as a space where Balzac can record the array of *objets d'art* he purchased for his future home, hoping to impress Madame Hanska; and lastly, the letters themselves are a cherished collection that can be locked away, handled, revisited — and reread. The act of rereading is integral to Balzac's practices of creation and storytelling, the correspondence acting as a repository for his creative ideas.

What emerges from all this is that Balzac's correspondence with Éveline underscores his status of creator, and producer of narratives. This is contrary to some of
the accepted ideas of Madame Hanska as a somewhat malevolent, dominating figure
who allegedly forced Balzac to expend his creative energies in this correspondence,
to the detriment of his fiction.[45] Balzac's much-bemoaned 'inability', over the
many years of the correspondence, to persuade Éveline to marry him and follow
him to Paris, has been viewed by some readers of the correspondence as something
of a failure. My monograph proposes a different view: from a detailed study of his
letters, we repeatedly see Balzac enjoying these literary constructs, and delighting in
the space for creative freedom which this relationship offers him. Frequently, Balzac
betrays no hurry to change the status quo and reduce the physical distance between
himself and his literary lover. Although Balzac's letters record his fantasies of being
close to his mistress, we can also clearly discern in them the kind of contentment
which Kaufmann identifies as a defining feature of many long-distance epistolary
relationships of writers, recognizing clear benefits to maintaining the correspondent
at a distance.[46] While writing love letters to his 'polar Star' which tell of his longing
for her, Balzac was satisfying his more urgent sexual needs elsewhere.[47]

That Balzac did not consider the correspondence with Éveline to be his one and
only source of pleasure (and therefore that he did not necessarily see his inability to
turn it into a marriage much earlier as a failure or disappointment) can be seen from
Balzac's letter to his sister Laure, dated 12 October 1833. In providing Laure with an
account of his first meeting with the tantalizing *Étrangère*, he described her thus:

> L'essentiel est que nous avons 27 ans, que nous sommes belle par admiration,
> que nous possédons les plus beaux cheveux noirs du monde, la peau suave et
> délicieusement fine des brunes, que nous avons une petite main d'amour, un
> cœur de 27 ans, naïf [...], je ne te parle pas des richesses colossales, qu'est-ce que
> c'est que cela devant un chef-d'œuvre de beauté [...]. J'ai été enivré d'amour.
> (*Corr*, I, 875)

> [The main thing is that we are 27 years old, that we are beautiful and admired,
> that we possess the most beautiful black hair in the world, as well as the smooth
> and deliciously fine skin of brunettes, that we have a tiny little hand made for
> love, a naive 27-year-old heart [...], I shan't even speak to you of colossal riches,
> what is that next to a masterpiece of beauty [...]. I was intoxicated with love.]

Yet Balzac's claim to overwhelming feelings of love is somewhat attenuated
by the very next lines of the letter, in which he paints a picture of his already
extraordinarily full love life:

> Je ne sais à qui conter cela, et certes ce n'est ni à *Elle*, la Grande Madame,
> la terrible Marquise [...]; ce n'est pas à *elle,* la pauvre, simple et délicieuse
> bourgeoise [...]. Ce n'est pas à *Elle,* la plus chérie, qui a encore plus de jalousie
> pour moi qu'une mère [...]; enfin, ce n'est pas à *elle,* qui veut sa ration d'amour
> journalière [...]; c'était donc à toi, ma bonne sœur, [...] que j'ai voulu conter ma
> joie. (*Corr*, I, 875–76)

> [I do not know to whom to tell this story, and certainly it shall not be to *Her*,
> the Grand Madame, the terrible Marquise [...]; nor to *her*, the poor, simple,
> delicious bourgeoise [...]. It shall not be to *Her*, the dearest one, who has even
> more jealousy towards me than a mother [...]; finally, it shall not be to *her*, who

wants her daily ration of love [...]; and so it was to you, my good sister, [...] that I have wanted to narrate my joy.]

Already from his remark 'Je ne sais à qui conter cela', we see that the liaison with Madame Hanska is, from the beginning, viewed at least in part as an excuse to create triumphant narratives. Moreover, the designation of Madame Hanska as 'nous' [we], side-by-side with a list of other women who are all juxtaposed to her by being referred to as 'elle' [her], reveals an attitude similar to that of a collector towards his array of pretty objects. In this letter, Madame Hanska is added to Balzac's 'harem',[48] and is differentiated from the list of other women only by the dubious distinction of the pronoun 'nous' — which from Balzac's wider writing would appear to be no distinction at all — and which, moreover, in this letter soon fades away into the long list of other women and their attributes.[49] In the light of this, it is necessary to reconsider what purpose the love correspondence with Éveline served for Balzac. It would be naïve to assume that he was just pursuing her for the purposes of marriage, and that Balzac would have considered the epistolary relationship as an inadequate substitute for the possibility of marriage. In fact, this correspondence supplies Balzac with a space in which to explore creative and narrative techniques and devices which later become interwoven with those in his fiction.

All this does not necessarily mean that Balzac did not fall in love with Éveline Hanska, nor that we can dismiss his love letters as not being based in genuine sentiment. An epistolary relationship of such long duration can naturally be expected to go through various highs and lows. That Balzac maintained the correspondence over so many years suggests more than just a cynical interest in yet another wealthy woman. Furthermore, it is precisely because of the literary benefits that Balzac derived from the correspondence that he went to great lengths both to maintain it and to preserve a large degree of control over it. We shall see some of the lengths to which he went in his letters in order to continue his relationship with Éveline — in his own way, by drawing on the ever-expanding wealth of resources available to him from his literary imagination.

Notes to the Introduction

1. *LMH*, I, 14 (7 November 1832).
2. For details of the first meeting, see *LMH*, I, 59, n. 2. See also Roger Pierrot, *Ève de Balzac* (Paris: Stock, 1999), pp. 71–76.
3. See *LMH*, I, 126, n. 1. Balzac's letters are somewhat coy, especially early on, when it comes to the sexual side of the relationship; only rarely does the discerning reader find a hint of suggestive innuendo — as in the following extract, where Balzac pictures 'mon cœur [...] dans ton cœur, ma pensée dans tes beaux cheveux, et ma bouche, je n'ose dire' [my heart [...] in your heart, my thoughts in your beautiful hair, and my mouth, I dare not say] (*LMH*, I, 140 [21 February 1834]). In later years, Balzac used references to a 'Bengali' — a little oriental bird, straining to escape his cage — when talking about sexual arousal.
4. See for example Roger Pierrot, *Honoré de Balzac* (Paris: Fayard, 1994); Gonzague Saint Bris, *Je vous aime inconnue: Balzac et Éva Hanska* (Paris: NiL, 1999); Emmanuel Dufour-Kowalski, *Balzac et madame Hanska: reminiscences d'un roman d'amour* (Paris: Panthéon, 1994); Graham Robb, *Balzac: A Biography* (London: Picador, 1994); Jacques Delaye, *Madame Honoré de Balzac* (Paris: Perrin, 1989); and Marcel Bouteron, *La Véritable Image de Madame Hanska* (Paris: Lapina, 1929).
5. Gustave Flaubert, *Correspondance*, in *Œuvres complètes*, ed. by Maurice Bardèche, 16 vols (Paris: Club de l'Honnête Homme, 1971), xv, 586, letter to Madame Roger des Genettes (August 1877).

6. For an analysis of Balzac's allusions to his (masculine) 'travaux' and to himself as (effeminate) 'poète', see Roland Le Huenen and Paul Perron, 'Les Lettres à Madame Hanska: métalangage du roman et représentation du romanesque', *Revue des sciences humaines*, 195 (1984), 25–40.

7. Roger Pierrot, 'Préface', *LMH*, I, III.

8. 'Voici bientôt dix ans que je vous écris sans relire mes phrases, et sans en avoir jamais fait une' [For almost ten years now I have been writing to you without rereading my words, and without ever specially overworking them] (*LMH*, I, 583–84, 2 June 1842); 'Je vous écris avec un abandon qui pourrait cependant m'inspirer de la crainte' [I write to you with an abandon that could well worry me] (*LMH*, I, 601, 25 August 1842); 'tout ce que vous avez reçu de moi, est-il si spontané que vous avez dû remarquer des redites' [everything you have received from me is so spontaneous that you must have noticed repetitions] (*LMH*, I, 624, 20 December 1842).

9. Balzac does mention 'lettres que j'ai brûlées, par peur de vous déplaire' [letters I have burnt, for fear of displeasing you] (*LMH*, I, 44, 19 July 1833); at other times, he admits to writing with a certain restraint. See *LMH*, I, 621 (7 December 1842).

10. Catherine Kerbat-Orecchioni, *Les Interactions verbales* (Paris: Collin, 1990), p. 14, cited in Ruth Amossy, 'La Lettre d'amour du réel au fictionnel', in *La Lettre entre réel et fiction*, ed. by Jürgen Siess (Paris: SEDES, 1998), pp. 73–96 (p. 77).

11. Honoré de Balzac, *Correspondance*, ed. by Roger Pierrot and Hervé Yon, 2 vols (Paris: Gallimard, 2006–11) (hereafter *Corr*), II, 41–42 (April 1836). There is no question mark in the original. On Balzac's quirks of spelling and punctuation, see Pierrot, 'Préface', *LMH*, I, XXI.

12. Honoré de Balzac, *La Comédie humaine*, ed. by Pierre-Georges Castex, 12 vols (Paris: Gallimard, Bibliotheque de la Pléiade, 1976–81) (hereafter *CH*), I, 541. This quotation is discussed in Franc Schuerewegen, *Balzac contre Balzac: les cartes du lecteur* (Toronto: SEDES/Paratexte, 1990), p. 121.

13. Amélie Schweiger, 'La Lettre d'orient', *Revue des sciences humaines*, 195 (1984), 41–57 (p. 41).

14. Amossy, p. 74.

15. Vincent Kaufmann, *L'Équivoque épistolaire* (Paris: Minuit, 1990), p. 8.

16. Anne-Marie Baron, *Balzac ou l'auguste mensonge* (Paris: Nathan, 1998), p. 60. See also José-Luis Diaz, 'A quoi servent les correspondances: l'exemple de Balzac', in *Pour Balzac et pour les livres: hommage à Roger Pierrot*, ed. by Thierry Bodin (Paris: Klincksieck, 1999), pp. 31–40, on the general functions of Balzac's wider correspondence.

17. See Kaufmann's introductory chapter, 'Reading in Bed', in *Post Scripts: The Writer's Workshop*, trans. by Deborah Treisman (Cambridge, MA, & London: Harvard University Press, 1994), pp. 1–13.

18. *LMH*, I, 393 (19 July 1837).

19. *LMH*, I, 470 (15 November 1838).

20. See José Luis Diaz, 'Naître par correspondance', in *Devenir Balzac: l'invention de l'écrivain par lui-même* (Saint-Cyr-sur-Loire: Christian Pirot, 2007), pp. 15–27.

21. See Owen Heathcote, '(Auto-)portrait d'un auteur en courtisane: le travail du sexe et le sexe du travail dans les Lettres à Mme Hanska', in *Paratextes balzaciens: 'La Comédie humaine' en ses marges*, ed. by Roland Le Huenen and Andrew Oliver (Toronto: Centre d'études du XIXe siècle Joseph Sable, 2007), pp. 179–90. Le Huenen & Perron, 'Les Lettres à Madame Hanska', pp. 25–40.

22. *LMH*, I, 522 (16 December 1840).

23. I discuss this theme in my article on instances of literary communication, 'An Aesthetics of Indirection in Novels and Letters: Balzac's Communication with Évelina Hanska', in *The Ethics of Literary Communication: Genuineness, Directness, Indirectness*, ed. by Roger Sell, Adam Borch and Inna Lindgren (Amsterdam: John Benjamins, 2013), pp. 229–46.

24. See for example Pierrot, 'Préface', *LMH*, I, IV–V.

25. See for example Anne-Marie Meininger's critique of the later years of the correspondence, in *CH*, VII, 15–16. See also Gérard Peylet, 'De la manie à la mélancolie: les souffrances du créateur balzacien dans la correspondance et dans les romans de 1830', *Eidôlon*, 52 (1999), 147–60, and 'Les souffrances du créateur: de la pathologie à la Passion dans les *Lettres à Madame Hanska* de Balzac', *Eidôlon*, 50 (1997), 323–30.

26. See Roger Pierrot, *Honoré de Balzac* (Paris: Fayard, 1994), p. 504, and Graham Robb, *Balzac: A Biography* (London: Picador, 1994), pp. 406–07.

27. Anne McCall Saint-Saëns, 'De la haine épistolaire ou "la fatale puissance de la lettre"', in *L'Érotique balzacienne*, ed. by Lucienne Frappier-Mazur and Jean-Marie Roulin (Paris: SEDES, 2001), pp. 41–50.

28. Uwe Vogel, *Balzac als Briefschreiber: ein Romancier zwischen Realität und Fiktion* (Frankfurt am Main: Haag & Herchen, 1986), p. 38.

29. See Brigitte Diaz, *Stendhal en sa correspondance, ou 'L'Histoire d'un esprit'* (Paris: Champion, 2003), p. 15. Diaz borrows this formulation from the title of Philippe Lejeune's work, *Les Brouillons de soi* (Paris: Seuil, 1998).

30. See *LMH*, I, 6.

31. I borrow the phrase from Stéphane Vachon, 'Un manuscrit dans une robe', in *Balzac: une poétique du roman*, ed. by Stéphane Vachon (Saint-Denis: Presses Universitaires de Vincennes, 1996), pp. 321–29 (p. 322).

32. Brigitte Diaz, *L'Épistolaire ou la pensée nomade: formes et fonctions de la correspondance dans quelques parcours d'écrivains au XIXe siècle* (Paris: PUF, 2002), p. 68.

33. See for example Balzac's letter dated 6 October 1833, written after Balzac has seen Éveline for the first time, *LMH*, I, 60–63.

34. Kaufmann, *L'Équivoque épistolaire*, p. 16.

35. Heathcote, '(Auto-)portrait d'un auteur en courtisane', p. 181.

36. *CH*, III, 148. This comment has been somewhat taken out of context by Baron, in her otherwise excellent study of 'échanges de lettres' in *La Comédie humaine* (*Balzac ou les hiéroglyphes de l'imaginaire* (Paris: Honoré Champion, 2002), p. 101). As we have seen in the already-cited extract from *Modeste Mignon* (*CH*, I, 541) (see above, n. 12), Balzac did not necessarily seek to represent all correspondence as being the 'soul' of its writer.

37. See Roland Barthes, *S/Z* (Paris: Seuil, 1970), pp. 22–23. See also Barbara Johnson, 'The Critical Difference: Barthes/BalZac', in *The Critical Difference: Essays in the Contemporary Rhetoric of Reading* (Baltimore, MD, & London: Johns Hopkins University Press, 1980), pp. 3–12 (p. 5).

38. *CH*, XI, 1019. On this concept, see José-Luis Diaz, 'Créer peut-être à deux', *L'Année balzacienne* (2010), 39–58.

39. I borrow the metaphor of 'haunting' from Matei Calinescu, *Rereading* (New Haven, CT, & London: Yale University Press, 1993), pp. xi-xii.

40. See Roger Pierrot, *LMH*, I, 13, n. 3.

41. See *LMH*, II, 548–73. On p. 572, n. 1, Pierrot notes: 'Toute cette affaire du vol des lettres, émaillée de contrevérités et de contradictions, nous laisse une impression de malaise' [This whole business of the theft of the letters, peppered with contradictions and counter-truths, leaves us feeling uneasy].

42. *LMH*, II, 681 (3 September 1847).

43. See David Bellos, 'Balzac and Goethe's Bettina', in *Literary Communication and Reception*, Innsbrucker Beiträge zur Kulturwissenschaft, Sonderheft 46 (Innsbruck: AMCE, 1980), pp. 359–64. Terence Cave has also commented on the influence of Bettina von Arnim's published correspondence on *Modeste Mignon*. See Terence Cave, *Mignon's Afterlives: Crossing Cultures from Goethe to the Twenty-First Century* (Oxford: Oxford University Press, 2011), p. 101.

44. It has not been possible, however, to retain a chronological approach throughout, for example with relation to the order of appearance of Balzac's novels in this monograph.

45. See for example *CH*, VII, 15–16, where, in her introduction to *La Cousine Bette* (1846) Meininger criticizes Balzac's later relationship with Madame Hanska, claiming that the letters stopped resembling a 'love' correspondence, and that they consumed his creative energies without any reward. However, Meininger's introductory pages also concede that, in this continued correspondence, Balzac found great creative inspiration for *La Cousine Bette*.

46. Kaufmann, *Post Scripts*, p. 21.

47. See *LMH*, II, 299 (12 August 1846), where Balzac confessed to having had other sexual partners during the epistolary relationship with Madame Hanska.

48. The metaphor of the harem was later used by Balzac himself, in relation to a collection in *Le Cousin Pons* (1847). See *CH*, VII, 597. This reference is discussed by John Patrick Greene, 'Balzac's Most Helpless Heroine: The Art Collection in *Le Cousin Pons*', *The French Review*, 69 (October 1995), 13–23 (p. 15).

49. Balzac closes the *Physiologie du mariage* with the following quotation from Brillat-Savarin: 'Quand j'écris et parle de moi au singulier, cela suppose une confabulation avec le lecteur; il peut examiner, discuter, douter, et même rire; mais, quand je m'arme du redoutable NOUS, je professe, il faut se soumettre' [When I write and talk about myself in the singular, this presupposes a confabulation with the reader; he can examine, discuss, doubt, even laugh; but when I arm myself with the formidable WE, I profess, the reader must submit] (*CH*, XI, 912). This quotation is briefly discussed by Baron, in *Balzac ou l'auguste mensonge*, p. 62.

CHAPTER 1

❖

The Blank Page and the Palimpsest

Je me créai une femme, je la dessinai dans ma pensée, je la rêvai.

[I fashioned myself a woman, I sketched her in my thoughts; I dreamed her.]

BALZAC, *La Peau de chagrin* (*CH*, X, 146)

In Laurence Sterne's *Tristram Shandy* (1759–67), a text which Balzac greatly admired, at one point the narrator offers his readers a blank page on which they are invited to draw, in order to arrive at their own understanding of the story — thus acknowledging the impossibility of expressing everything through words. Specifically, the blank page is provided for them so that they may use it to draw their ideal woman:

> To conceive this right — call for pen and ink — here's paper ready to your hand. — Sit down, Sir, paint her to your own mind — as like your mistress as you can — as unlike your wife as your conscience will let you — 'tis all one to me — please but your own fancy in it.[1]

Possibly Balzac was drawing some inspiration from this text when in 1833 he remarked on Hanska's tendency to leave the odd blank page amidst the handwritten pages of her letters: 'Pourquoi me laissez-vous des pages blanches dans vos lettres. Mais laissez, laissez. Rien de forcé. Ce blanc, moi je le remplis. Je me dis que votre bras a passé là et je baise le blanc' [Why do you keep leaving me blank pages in your letters. But go ahead, leave them. I fill this blank myself. I tell myself that your arm passed over it and I kiss the white space].[2]

Exactly why Madame Hanska should have left blank pages in her letters (repeatedly, it would seem) will never be known. It is tempting to imagine that she left them there intentionally, and to interpret her gesture of sending blank pages as creative and meaningful (as some scholars already have done).[3] It is exciting to think that Hanska may have been somehow calling on him to write. After all, she was writing to one of her favourite authors — and she had already expressed her intention to help him become a great writer. Perhaps it was she, and not he, who was assuming the role of Tristram Shandy.

Or perhaps she simply picked up a few extra sheets from a stack of paper, and enclosed them by accident. We shall never know. Her blank pages are noteworthy, in fact, because Balzac himself comments upon them and invests them with significance; and this is arguably demonstrative and illustrative of his, not Éveline's, creative imagination.

In the absence of any tangible details of the correspondent — with no clue as to her physical appearance, the sound of her voice, or indeed any concrete information about her character, preferences, or personality — Balzac pounces on the rich symbolic potential of Madame Hanska's blank pages. We can view the blank page as a metaphor for the way in which Balzac creates an imaginary 'Eve' from the blank canvas that the (quite possibly accidental) page presents him with. We shall also see how Balzac further explores this process of creating and imagining a character from a minimal base of real-world evidence in his novels, in particular in *Le Médecin de campagne*, through the character of 'Évelina'. Several of Balzac's 'Pygmalion stories' (such as *Le Chef-d'œuvre inconnu* (1831), *La Maison du chat-qui-pelote* (1830), and *Sarrasine*), show in greater detail how the process of character creation, and its link to the desires and fantasies of the creator, fascinates and preoccupies him. As for the correspondence with Madame Hanska, the letters which date from May 1832 (the beginning of the correspondence) to 18 September 1833 (the last letter before the pair met for the first time, in Neuchâtel) are particularly fascinating, as the *Étrangère* is almost entirely unknown to Balzac, and his understanding of her character is to a large extent a figment of his imagination at this stage.

To a writer, a blank page has a particular symbolic weight. It can be associated with writer's block — which in French is rendered as 'la hantise de la page blanche' [the obsessive fear of the blank page]. It is striking that, while in the English phrase 'writer's block' the problem is on the side of the *writer*, the French expression implies that it is the blank page itself which is tormenting the writer and which is the source of the difficulty. Balzac thus belongs to a linguistic tradition in which the blank page exerts a form of power over the person who confronts it. This may help explain why he views the blank page as such an important symbol. On most of the occasions when Balzac's letters make reference to blank pages, it is to complain about his inability to produce text. At one time he refers to his fruitless endeavours as 'l'enfer de l'encrier et du papier blanc' [the hell of the inkwell and the white paper].[4] Another time, he writes, 'Je ne sais rien de plus lassant que d'être resté pendant toute une nuit, [...] devant son papier blanc, sans rien trouver' [I do not know of anything more tiring than to have remained up all night, [...] in front of one's blank paper, and not find anything].[5] For Balzac the creative writer, then, the blank page can be a negative preoccupation, a source of anxiety and fear.

Yet the blank pages sent by Hanska do not seem to have any of these connotations, and become transformed into a playful symbol of creativity and expression. The blank page has the potential to be even more powerful than a page filled with writing; containing everything that is as yet unwritten, and free of the constraints of a text, it allows Balzac to project onto it whatever vision he wants (in the words of Susan Gubar, 'the blank page contains all stories in no story, just as silence contains all potential sound and white contains all color').[6]

Like Sterne's ideal, imagined woman, Balzac's also defies a verbal representation. As Barthes suggests, falling in love is a visual act, in the sense that one initially falls in love with a tableau — a visual picture, or a staged scene.[7] By this we can understand that the love object — at least, as presented by the western literary canon — initially appears as a more or less complete, 'metaphorically framed', picture.[8] In several of Balzac's artist stories, the moment of falling in love likewise occurs when the love object is perceived as a kind of painting, framed by a window frame, for example, or set off to his or her best advantage by the objects and the environment that surround him or her. In *La Maison du chat-qui-pelote,* the artist who perceives the girl through a window is struck by the beauty of the complete tableau, and then goes on to paint an actual picture of her. In *Albert Savarus,* Rosalie sees Albert through the window and contemplates him as if he were a silent tableau. In keeping with Barthes's observation, it is with such a tableau, with a self-contained and somewhat idealized vision of the other, that the artist falls in love — a point stressed by Balzac's stories, in which the artist-voyeur subsequently attempts to recreate that initial vision through art.

In the case of Balzac's own relationship with Madame Hanska, where the initial contact was by letter, Balzac was offered no such tableau of her with which to fall in love; instead, he 'painted' it himself. In the letters to Hanska, as in Sterne's text, the blank page becomes a space of visual representation. Balzac's evocation of his mysterious correspondent is necessarily impressionistic and sketchy; he cannot presume to tell her what she might look like, and so his letters convey only imagined fragments of her. For example, Balzac conjures up the hands which handle the gift he sent her — 'Il est si doux de se dire: Elle touche et ouvre une petite cassette que voici!' [How sweet it is to tell yourself: She is touching and opening this little box!] — and an image of the white arm which glides over the white paper, becoming one with the blank page.[9] The white underside of the arm (in French, *le blanc du bras*) and the white of the paper seem to merge in the erotically-charged image of Balzac kissing 'le blanc' [the white space].[10]

The *Étrangère* thus becomes a part of the literary process, a 'blank' to be filled in; the writing paper becomes a repository for love and for caresses in place of the absent arm. Moreover, Balzac's caress appears to be a creative action, much in the same way that the caress has been represented in modern theory and literature.[11] When he writes 'je ne vous verrai peut-être jamais, vous que je caresse comme une illusion, qui êtes dans tous mes rêves comme une espérance, et qui avez si gracieusement donné un corps à mes rêveries' [perhaps I will never see you, you whom I caress as an illusion, you who are in all my dreams like a kind of hope, and who have so graciously given a body to my reveries],[12] Balzac suggests that his metaphorical caress deliberately and knowingly fashions (or, to borrow Sartre's phrase, '[fait] naître', or gives life to) his correspondent.[13]

Balzac's early letters to his *Étrangère*, during the period when he is essentially 'creating' her, vividly recall the myth of Pygmalion. In Ovid's version of this myth, Pygmalion created the statue of a woman, one which was so beautiful that he quickly fell in love with his creation; he dressed and undressed her, and slept with her at night:

> In gorgous [*sic*] garments, furthermore, he did her also deck
> And on her fingers put he rings and chains about her neck. [...]
> All kind of things became her well. And when she was undressed
> She seemed not less beautiful.[14]

Through the intervention of the goddess Venus, the statue was finally transformed into a flesh-and-blood woman. This myth, which, as Balzac scholars have already demonstrated, has a strong resonance in several of his works, also has a strong echo in some of Balzac's allusions to the unknown *Étrangère*.[15] The sexual yet also creative caress of the artist's hand, the notion of giving a body to a fantasy, are just two possible examples. When he makes a subtle allusion to 'dressing' his correspondent — 'Je vous ai donc *revêtue* de toutes ces idées' [Thus I have dressed you anew in all these ideas][16] — Balzac is rather like his fictional Pygmalions.[17] His subtle erotic reference reflects some of the more salacious 'dressing up' scenarios in his novels. There is Frenhofer, for instance, who insists that his painted mistress is not 'dressed' and therefore cannot leave his studio: 'Née dans mon atelier, elle [...] n'en peut sortir que vêtue. La poésie et les femmes ne se livrent nues qu'à leurs amants!' [Born in my studio, she [...] must not leave it unless she is clothed. Poetry and women only give themselves naked to their lovers!] (*CH*, x, 431); and Sarrasine, who is described mentally unveiling his model Zambinella as he sketches picture after picture of her imagined, perfect forms (see *CH*, vi, 1062). We might also think of Raphaël de Valentin in *La Peau de chagrin*, mentally dressing up the innocent Pauline in the finery required by society, in order to see her as attractive ('Combien de fois n'ai-je pas vêtu de satin les pieds mignons de Pauline, emprisonné sa taille svelte [...] dans une robe de gaze, jeté sur son sein une légère écharpe [...]; je l'eusse adorée ainsi' [How many times did I not dress Pauline's darling feet in satin, imprison her svelte waist [...] in a gauze dress, throw a light shawl over her breast [...]; I would have adored her like that], *CH*, x, 143). A further example of dressing up — and something of a reversal of the traditional gender roles — is Paquita Valdès in *La Fille aux yeux d'or*, who delights in dressing Henri de Marsay in a woman's scarf, bonnet, and clothes as a prelude to sex. In Balzac's novels, allusions to the 'dressing' or 'undressing' of the love object indicate a prolonged act of intimacy between would-be artists and their imagined creations.

As the love correspondence progressed, Balzac declined to see Éveline's portrait, saying 'je ne le veux qu'après vous avoir vue' [I do not want it until after I have seen you].[18] He thus suggested that it was *his* creativity which was driving his vision of her and which should not be disrupted by extraneous objects. Balzac the writer preferred to build his own picture of the correspondent's 'figure douce' [sweet face] and 'formes attrayantes' [attractive forms] — 'la douceur' [sweetness] being, of course, a subjective quality, as is attractiveness.[19] He did not seek to attribute any objectively verifiable qualities to the face and form of Éveline, preferring to super-impose his own subjective criteria onto them, and taking great care not to have his vision contradicted. Like Pygmalion, he wished to create in order to possess.

Balzac's description of the *Étrangère* is a mixture of the statuesque and the physical on the one hand, and of the vague and ungraspable on the other. 'Vous ne vous moquerez pas de moi', he wrote in January 1833. 'Vous êtes une des figures idéales auxquelles j'ai laissé le droit de venir parfois se poser nuageusement devant mes fleurs, et qui me sourient entre deux camélias, agitent mes bruyères roses, et auxquelles je parle?' [You will not make fun of me [...]. You are one of those ideal figures whom I have occasionally permitted to come and lie down mistily before my flowers, and who smile at me from between two camellias, who disturb my pink heathers, and to whom I speak?].[20] While the woman is here represented in spatial terms — she approaches the writer, sits down, flowers are shaken as she brushes past, or settles down nearby (perhaps lies down?) — at the same time, the image of her smiling 'between two camellias' suggests that Balzac is envisaging a tableau, glimpsing the woman as being surrounded or partially concealed by flowers. Although (like Pygmalion's sculpted woman) she fills a three-dimensional space and has a palpably physical presence, on some level she remains inaccessible.[21] The writer speaks *to* her; yet there is no question of a response. The 'ideal figure' is tantalizingly close, yet partially obscured; she is communicative, yet silent. The suggestion that Balzac gives the figure permission to approach — and only 'occasionally' — makes clear that he, Pygmalion, is in control. (Also, following my earlier discussion of Balzac's preference for having numerous female correspondents, it is interesting that Balzac refers to Éveline as '*one* of those figures'.)

To continue to evoke his correspondent in vague and undefined terms seems to him to have been preferable to being able to picture her clearly. Unlike his fictional Pygmalions, who are on a quest to find and then visually represent a perfect female figure, Balzac suggests, in his letters, that to be enjoying the unknown stranger at a distance is in fact preferable to encountering her in the flesh:

> Je suis comme un prisonnier qui, du fond de son cachot, entend au loin, une délicieuse voix de femme. Il porte toute son âme dans les fragiles et puissantes perceptions de cette voix, et après ses longues heures de rêverie, d'espérances, après les voyages de son imagination, la femme, belle, jeune, le tuerait, tant le bonheur serait complet.[22]

> [I am like a prisoner who, from the depths of his dungeon, hears from afar a woman's delicious voice. He puts his entire soul into the fragile and powerful perceptions of this voice, and after his long hours of daydreaming, of hoping, after the voyages of his imagination, the woman, beautiful and young, would kill him, for his happiness would be so complete.]

'Ce que nous peignons est fini, déterminé' [What we paint is finished, determined], Balzac wrote when comparing the plight of the writer with that of the musician, whose chosen medium allows him (or so Balzac believes) to represent the 'infini' [infinite].[23] In picturing Madame Hanska only in an incomplete, even fragmented form — that is, by avoiding 'finishing' her or gaining the knowledge that would allow him to complete his picture of her — the novelist seems deliberately to avoid the 'finished' and the 'determined', and thereby instead continues to enjoy the infinite potential of imagining the unknown. As Balzac observed in *Modeste Mignon,* 'L'inconnu, c'est l'infini obscur, et rien n'est plus attachant' [The unknown is infinite and obscure, and nothing could be more appealing] (*CH*, I, 540).

An analysis of Balzac's first letter to Madame Hanska (written in May 1832) shows to what extent his way of imagining her was linked to literary creation:

> Madame, je vous supplie de séparer complètement l'auteur de l'homme, et de croire à la sincérité des sentiments que j'ai dû exprimer vaguement [...]. Si vous daignez excuser la folie d'un cœur jeune, et d'une imagination toute vierge, je vous avouerai que vous avez été pour moi l'objet des plus doux rêves. En dépit de mes travaux, je me suis surpris plus d'une fois, chevauchant à travers les espaces et voltigeant dans la contrée inconnue où vous, inconnue, habitiez seule de votre race.[24]

> [Madam, I beg you to separate the man from the writer completely, and to believe in the sincerity of those feelings which I must have expressed rather vaguely [...]. If you would deign to excuse the folly of a young heart, and of a virgin imagination, I will admit that you have been the object of some of my sweetest dreams. In spite of my work I have surprised myself on more than one occasion, straddling immense distances and flying to the unknown country where you, also unknown, live as the only representative of your race.]

Balzac asks the *Étrangère* nothing about herself; instead, he describes his pleasurable flights of fancy as he pictures her amongst the 'restes [...] malheureux [d'un] peuple dispersé' [unhappy remnants of a dispersed people] calling out to him across immense distances.[25] This is an imaginative allusion to Goethe's Romantic notion of elective affinities, an idea which had general currency at the time.[26] Balzac seems to have been genuinely interested in the concept of dispersion of molecules; he wondered in his *Notes philosophiques* 'Quelle est la puissance coercitive qui retient et assemble les molécules ou parties des substances matérielles?' [What is the power which holds and assembles molecules and parts of material substances?] (*CH*, x, 1642, n. 6) and explored this idea in *La Recherche de l'absolu* (*CH*, x, 720). (By the time Flaubert exploited the concept of elective affinities in *Madame Bovary* (1856) in a farcical way during the scene of the agricultural show, as part of Rodolphe's seduction of Emma, the idea was thoroughly out of fashion.)[27]

Significantly, in 1835, Balzac linked the concepts of 'atoms' (*atomes crochus*), affinities and correspondence in *Le Père Goriot*: describing a letter as a 'soul', he suggested a connection between letters and elective affinities, insofar as feelings *can* travel across immense distances — in the form of letters (*CH*, III, 148). Arguably, this link between correspondence and elective affinities had first been made in his earliest letter to the *Étrangère*; her letters, flying to him across immense distances, are like the 'âme' [soul], or 'écho de la voix qui parle' [echo of the voice that speaks] to which he refers in *Le Père Goriot* (Ibid.). The letters themselves thus play a part in this fantasy of reuniting scattered, exiled peoples. From the outset, Balzac set the correspondence in the realm of the 'romanesque' [novelistic], with himself at the helm of this creative fantasy; and secondly, the idea of molecules entering a melting pot to re-emerge as part of a new entity (which is at the heart of the notion of elective affinities), of a re-creation following the effacement of something old, hints at Balzac's desire to use this correspondence to efface his previous 'origins' and to re-create himself in this new epistolary relationship.[28]

This first letter has a strong literary quality — unsurprising, perhaps, if we consider the bibliophilic impetus that brought them together (Madame Hanska had read and admired his novels). To an extent, Balzac is even echoing the narrative voice of his fictional work: in begging her to separate the author and the work, he is directly echoing fragments of a similar appeal to the reader in the famous 'Préface' to the first edition of *La Peau de chagrin* (1831), in which he warned against the reader's tendency to impose preconceived judgments onto authors, and complained of his own unfair treatment by his readers.[29] However, the literary quality of this letter, and the way it self-consciously lays claim to originality, alerts us to another function of this correspondence. It is one thing that Balzac should allude to their shared literary understanding, or that he should strive to represent himself as a great writer and use his literary skill to create a bond between himself and his correspondent; Balzac also appears to use his first letter to an unknown correspondent to try to 'create' her and her origin from scratch. The early letters, which revolve around notions of authenticity and originality, in fact constitute a reworking of past correspondence and of the writer's past life.

The kind of pact that Balzac wants to enter into with Madame Hanska includes an implicit agreement about what constitutes an 'authentic' origin. If Madame Hanska is to accept Balzac's narrative, and thus enter into a relationship, she will be required, in effect, to 'efface' existing origins and fabricate new ones that chime with Balzac's discourse of authenticity. As we shall see, the correspondence with

Éveline was not at all 'original' to Balzac; he was reworking past correspondence and reusing techniques which he had used in previous relationships. Balzac tried to reinforce the notion that the relationship with Éveline pre-dated all other relationships; yet within the text itself there are clear indications that it is impossible to start completely from scratch.

The idea that a destruction or dismantling of something old is a vital prelude to creation has a strong resonance in Balzac's fiction. In *La Recherche de l'absolu* (1834), Balthazar Claës argues against the view that 'Décomposer n'est pas créer' [Decomposing is not creating] and claims that destruction is a vital part of creation (*CH*, x, 720). Balzac himself was famous for continually rewriting, reworking, and attempting to perfect his works, covering his proofs with so many scribbles that editors detested reading them, and envisaging new and different drafts of them even after they had already been 'magnifiquement imprimés' [printed magnificently].[30] We also know that he used his literary work to rewrite *himself*; in the preface to *La Dernière Fée ou la nouvelle lampe merveilleuse* [The Last Fairy or the New Magical Lamp] (1823), which was among the last of his early novels, the reader witnesses the death of 'Horace de Saint-Aubin' (Balzac's pseudonym up until that time) and the introduction of the illustrious 'Honoré de Balzac' (the name under which his works were later published).[31]

In the story, Horace goes into a white house, where he encounters Balzac — 'un jeune homme qui achevait les *Scènes de la vie privée* et *La Physiologie du mariage*' [a young man who was just finishing the *Scènes de la vie privée* and *La Physiologie du mariage*), who receives him 'comme un frère' [like a brother] (*PR*, I, 1094). After dinner one evening, the two authors read one another extracts from their works: Horace reads part of *L'Excommunié*, the host obliges with the latest *Scènes de la vie privée*. After listening to his host, Horace is in despair:

> — Je vois bien, s'écria-t-il, que je ne suis qu'un misérable! Je brise ma plume et je rentre dans l'ombre d'où je n'aurais jamais dû sortir.
> Son ami essaya vainement de l'encourager; Horace n'écrivit plus une ligne. Ce fut sans doute le lendemain de cette soirée que je le trouvai dans la rue du Four, jetant ses romans aux flammes et incendiant le tuyau de sa cheminée. (*PR*, I, 1094–95)

> ['I can see very well,' he cried, 'that I am just a miserable wretch! I shall break my pen and go back to the obscurity that I never should have left.'
> In vain did his friend try to encourage him; Horace never wrote another line. It was no doubt the following day that I found him in the rue du Four, throwing his novels into the flames and setting his stovepipe on fire.]

Thus Balzac's novels actually record the moment of his 'becoming' Balzac, and obliterate less desirable past selves, exploring 'new' ones, but which are in fact a return to former ones; after all, in 'becoming' Honoré de Balzac, he was going from a nom de plume to the *nom du père* — the surname chosen by his father. (Bernard-François had himself changed his original surname, Balssa, to the more elegant-sounding Balzac, only occasionally adding the aristocratic 'de'.[32] By insisting on the permanent use of the particle 'de' — made manifest in his reply to Hanska's first extant letter, which he signed 'A l'É-h. de B.' instead of 'A l'É-h. B.' as per her instructions — the younger Balzac is building on his father's conscious use of renaming for social-climbing purposes.)[33]

Through his fiction, Balzac also creates multiple destinies for himself which allow him to rewrite and recreate his own story endlessly. We can consider both Louis Lambert and Félix de Vandenesse (the former a genius whose family life was untroubled, the latter an emotional youth whose early life has been blighted by a lack of maternal love) as avatars of Balzac's childhood self, their portrayal allowing him to explore several possible versions of himself. This aspect of Balzac's writing, which we might call 'palimpsestuous' — Balzac writes, and then starts again, the earlier version still partially visible through the new writing — informs also the writing of his letters, their 'coming into being', and their form.[34]

Throughout Balzac's palimpsestuous letter-writing, one can trace a constant tension between the desire for self-creation on the one hand, and the search for origins on the other. It is possible to trace the origins of Balzac's writing all the way back to his childhood, and to suggest that it begins in and springs from that original source which is the relationship with the mother. Balzac's multiple examples of correspondence with women represent his ceaseless attempts to reinvigorate, or recreate, the maternal relationship.

II

'Je suis né en 7bre 1833' [I was born in September 1833], Balzac later claimed to Madame Hanska, referring to the date of their first meeting.[35] Just as Balzac allows his literary persona to become 'reborn' through new writings, so he appears to believe that his relationship with this new correspondent does the same thing. However, through a study of Balzac's correspondence with Hanska, and of that with other women, it becomes apparent that what he claims to be a completely fresh start is, in fact, a series of constant repetitions and redraftings of this original relationship; his dream of immaculate self-conception ironically cannot but be shaped by the (absent) mother figure. This ceaseless process of remaking the old into something new is at the heart of Balzac's creativity.

Of his relationship with his mother, Balzac told Madame Hanska 'Je n'ai eu ni mère, ni enfance' [I had neither a mother, nor a childhood].[36] This crucial remark merits a detailed analysis. Balzac's childhood was characterized by the absence of his family and in particular of his mother, whom he seems to have feared and loved in equal measure. As a baby, he was sent out to a wet-nurse and subsequently left there for four years without ever seeing his parents during that time (a decision which, Laure Surville claimed, was made with Honoré's best interests at heart; the mother had lost her first child after trying to breastfeed it herself, and so, arguably, was doing her best to avoid making the same mistake).[37] He was then sent to the Collège Vendôme for seven years — a harrowing experience which left the young Balzac in a state of stupour.[38] It was the mother, as Laure Surville points out, who handed out any punishments or treats to the children, and it was to her that the young Balzac addressed his epistolary pleas of acceptance and of forgiveness for his misdemeanours.[39]

Balzac's earliest surviving letter to his mother, written in 1809, is a heartrending apology for his parents' disappointment in him — for which the young Honoré offers to make up by working diligently and cleaning his teeth:

> Je pense que mon papa a été désolé quand il a su que j'ai été à l'alcôve. Je te prie de le consoler en lui disant que j'ai eu un accessit. Je n'oublie pas de me frotter les dents avec mon mouchoir. J'ai fait un chayer [sic] où je recopie mes chayers nettement et j'ai des bons points et c'est de cette manière que je compte te faire plaisir. (Corr, 1, 3)[40]

> [I think my papa was sad when he learned that I had been in the alcove. Please make him feel better by telling him that I got a prize. I never forget to clean my teeth with my handkerchief. I made an exercise book where I copy out my exercise books in neat and it is in this way that I hope to please you.]

Throughout his life and his correspondence, Balzac betrayed a constant need for approbation from his mother. Writing in 1846 to Madame Hanska, whom he hoped to marry that year, Balzac writes, in the first instance: 'j'aurai sur moi mes actes en règle; celui de naissance, celui du décès de mon père et le consentement de ma mère' [I will have my documents in order; my birth certificate, my father's death certificate and my mother's written consent].[41] In a subsequent extract, he dwells again on the consent from his mother: 'il faut que j'aille faire préparer cet acte exigé par la loi jusqu'à 30 ans, mais qu'un fils respectueux fait à tout âge' [I must go and prepare this document, which is required by law for anyone under 30, but which a respectful son should procure at any age].[42] The repetition is significant, for it emphasizes the importance, to Balzac, of the idea of duty to the mother. These comments bring out the family dynamic which underlies Balzac's adult life: an absent father and a mother whose approval he strongly feels he must seek. Writing to his sister Laure in 1821, Balzac describes his father as 'la pyramide d'Égypte, immuable au milieu des éboulements du globe' [the Egyptian pyramid, immovable even with the world collapsing around it], while the mother is described as 'compensant par son activité l'immobilité de Papa' [making up for Papa's immobility with her activity] (Corr, 1, 74). The metaphor of the pyramid points to the physical and symbolic immobility — and towering size — of a quasi-reified father figure, while Balzac's mother compensates for the father's stasis.

While Balzac's letters to Madame Hanska frequently vilify his mother, some of his complaints against her are clear exaggerations; for instance, when, in writing of his financial problems, he claims that 'Ma mère m'a ruiné en 1827' [My mother ruined me in 1827], this is certainly untrue.[43] Similarly, his assertion that 'Ma mère est l'auteur de tous mes maux' [My mother is the author of all my troubles] is also an exaggeration.[44] Balzac is not consistent, in his letters to Madame Hanska, in the picture he paints of his mother; on one occasion, angry over some perceived slight from Madame Hanska, he writes her a letter in which he holds up this much-maligned mother as a paragon of love and care.[45]

Towards the end of his life, Balzac did genuinely come to a more charitable view of his mother; for years, however, he had reasons for feeling that his mother did not love him. 'Elle me hait pour bien des raisons, elle me haïssait avant que je fusse né' [She hates me for many reasons, she hated me even before I was born], he writes to

Hanska, referring apparently to the fact that his mother had lost a firstborn child, Louis-Daniel, born exactly a year before Balzac; thus he may well have been made to feel like an inadequate substitute, unable to ever compensate for the mother's loss.[46] Balzac's expulsion from the family home, according to Surville, was directly linked to this death; if Balzac's childhood was largely marred by the mother's decision to send him away, this decision seems to have been based on her loss of the firstborn child. In his notebook *Pensées, sujets, fragments*, Balzac makes an allusion to this when he writes, 'Je suis venu une heure trop tard au monde et je n'ai jamais pu rattraper cette heure-là' [I arrived in this world an hour too late, and I have never been able to catch up that one hour].[47]

Thus Balzac's early relationship with his mother, such as it existed, was conducted mainly through letter-writing (according to Baron, this explains his later-life propensity for letter-writing and for long-distance relationships, in which letters are substituted for physical proximity).[48] The one and only letter in existence written to the young Honoré by his mother dates back to 1814 and is a letter of chastisement, deploring his bad grades and announcing his punishment (*Corr*, I, 4).[49] This dynamic between mother and son — the son begging for approval which the mother withholds — is one which colours his lifelong correspondence with his mother, and indeed with other women.

There is an instance in Balzac's fiction where the link is drawn between early trauma and the compulsion to write letters. In *Le Lys dans la vallée,* the fictional protagonist Félix de Vandenesse invites a reflection on a childhood pattern of correspondence as he describes his schooldays, which are largely marred by the traumatic experience of writing letters which receive no satisfactory reply — only criticism from the mother, 'qui me réprimandait avec ironie sur mon style' [who reprimanded me sarcastically over my style] (*CH*, IX, 975):

> Pour décider mes parents à venir au collège, je leur écrivais des épîtres pleines de sentiments [...]. Je promettais de remplir les conditions que ma mère et mon père mettaient à leur arrivée, j'implorais l'assistance de mes sœurs [...]. Aux approches de la distribution des prix, je redoublais mes prières, je parlais de triomphes pressentis. (*CH*, IX, 975)

> [To convince my parents to come see me at school, I wrote them epistles full of feeling [...]. I promised to fulfil any conditions which my mother and father attached to their visit, I implored my sisters for assistance [...]. When prize-giving approached, I redoubled my prayers, I told them of my foreseen triumphs.]

This novel draws our attention to several potentially traumatic outcomes of attempting a correspondence. Writing sentimental letters exposes one to humiliation, as indeed Félix found when his heartfelt letters invited only ridicule from his mother. The content, or simply the absence or presence, of letters creates a space for ambiguity or misinterpretation, a gap that can be filled by desire or fantasy; Félix interprets the silence of his parents as the promise of his wish-fulfilment, attaching his own meaning to the silence which in fact signals only indifference, as the very next lines show:

> Trompé par le silence de mes parents, je les attendais en m'exaltant le cœur,

> je les annonçais à mes camarades; et quand, à l'arrivée des familles, le pas du vieux portier qui appelait les écoliers retentissait dans les cours, j'éprouvais alors des palpitations maladives. Jamais ce vieillard ne prononça mon nom. (*CH*, ix, 975)

> [Misled by my parents' silence, I awaited them with exhilaration, I told my classmates they were coming; and when, as the families were arriving, and the tread of the old porter who called out the pupils started to resound in the courtyards, I would start to feel sick with palpitations. Never did that old man pronounce my name.]

This fictional passage reflects Balzac's own experience to a large extent — initially in writing to his mother, and later in corresponding with Madame Hanska (who also apparently criticized Balzac's style, likening it to that of a 'collégien' [schoolboy],[50] and who sometimes left him without a reply).[51] This passage shows Balzac exploring, through the character of Félix, the effect of such a non-acknowledgment of the letter-writer's existence. The frantic flow of words produced by Félix — emphasized by the long sentences punctuated by the words 'j'écrivais', 'je promettais', 'j'implorais', 'je redoublais mes prières', 'je parlais', 'je les annonçais' — becomes almost a kind of logorrhoea, and, as we learn in the last short sentence, is met with silence. The anastrophe of this last sentence starting with 'Jamais' gives prominence to the fact that the letter-writer's existence is being radically denied; the non-utterance of his name symbolically deprives him of his identity — for to name is to bring someone into existence. Moreover, it shatters the self-protecting illusions that he had been cultivating up to this point, and the prestige he had been attempting to court among classmates. The letter from the parents would have resulted in a call to the letter-writer to come out into the real world and participate in real life. Without this call, he is instead condemned to 'ne vivre qu'en moi' [live only in myself] (*CH*, ix, 975); it is the mother who has the power to thus condemn him, or to grant him a pardon.

Why, then, would Balzac continue writing letters in adulthood, given his awareness of the potentially damaging outcomes that can result? Maintaining a pattern of correspondence throughout adulthood as Balzac does can be interpreted in several ways. It might be read, for example, as an unconscious or compulsive re-enactment of a traumatic experience. We can also view letter-writing as a soothing repetitive action, a regression into a safe place (for Freud, 'repetition, the re-experiencing of something identical, is clearly in itself a source of pleasure').[52] The experience of Félix suggests that whatever the response, the act of letter-writing is a comfort in itself, at least at the time of writing. It allows the letter-writer to nourish illusions and hope for a desired outcome. Although, as we know, the reply which the adult Félix eventually receives from Natalie de Manerville to his lengthy confession is a letter of rejection, it is nonetheless important for him to have written that confession. As Janet Beizer points out, the 'verbiage incessant' [incessant verbiage] of Félix can be seen to be the direct result of his abandonment by the mother.[53] Beizer cites Kristeva's somewhat abstract, poetical suggestion that the flow of words can be seen to replace the flow of the mother's milk: to release a flow of words is to nourish and build oneself up with them, having been denied such nourishment elsewhere. 'Par la bouche que je remplis des mots plutôt que de ma mère qui me manque désormais plus que jamais, j'élabore ce manque, et l'agressivité qui l'accompagne, en *disant'* [Through my mouth, which I fill with words rather than with my mother's milk, which I now miss more than ever, I elaborate on this lack, and the aggressivity that comes with it, by *saying*].[54]

Letter-writing, then, can be seen as a form of mastery, an attempt at positive self-creation. The young letter-writer in the passage is constantly trying to rework himself: he goes from writing 'épîtres pleines de sentiments' [epistles full of feeling] to writing about his 'triomphes pressentis' [foreseen triumphs]. This particular attempt on the part of Félix results in a sense of failure; however, the letter-writer can make renewed efforts, as indeed Félix does at later stages in his life, in writing to new and multiple correspondents, increasing the chances that someone might reply.

Like the fictional Félix, Balzac was neglected in favour of a preferred sibling. Balzac's younger brother, Henry, the adulterine child of his mother and Jean de Margonne, became the mother's clear favourite (a favourite who, later in life, would turn out to be a source of constant worry to her).[55] This formative experience has considerable resonance with the way in which Balzac interacts with Éveline Hanska and the patterns of naming that are employed in the correspondence, impacting also on Balzac's processes of textual creation.

Graham Robb points out in his biography of Balzac that the name of this second son, with its fashionable, English ending 'y' rather than the more common 'i', is like an improvement on the similar-sounding name Honoré; Henry (significantly, a child born out of a love affair) may be seen as an improved, younger, more desirable version of the first son, Honoré (a child of duty, we might say, born out of a less harmonious relationship).[56] To this suggestion, I would also add that, if we can view the names Henry and Honoré in this way, we can also note significant similarities between the names of the daughters of Madame Balzac. The elder sister was given the same name as the mother, Laure; the younger daughter — as though she were a 'version', a diminution, of the elder — was christened Laurence. The daughters' names are almost like declensions of the original name of the mother. This underscores the fact that, in a biblical sense, she *is* the origin, and her daughters are derivations of her; she has authorship of her children, as demonstrated through these nominal signifiers, and she reserves the right to give or take away life. We note that in 1846 Balzac tells Madame Hanska that his mother 'a tué Laurence' [killed Laurence].[57] This refers to the untimely death of the youngest sister, which resulted largely from the exhaustion and financial worry caused by her ill-advised marriage, which Balzac appears to blame on his mother. The idea that the mother 'killed' her daughter reminds one of Balzac's comment about his mother being the 'author' of all the misfortunes in his life. In a sense, her children and their lives are her 'works' (suggesting an almost divine form of authorship) and that she can dispose of them as she sees fit.

It is striking that Balzac's early childhood should be characterized by this sense of himself as an imperfect 'draft', a 're-writing'. An inadequate substitute for the lost son, Louis-Daniel, he himself becomes 'replaced' by another, much more desirable substitute, Henry (and, as we have seen, this implicit parental preference is reinforced even through nominal signifiers — that is to say, through the younger brother's very name). In his fiction, Balzac later 'avenges' his younger self by using similar processes to the ones learned in childhood, by which he disposes of inadequate 'younger brothers' (we witnessed such a process at work briefly in the example of Horace de Saint Aubin; Rose Fortassier offers a rich analysis of Henry's various literary deaths).[58] This notion of people as 'drafts', based on his early experience with names, is crucial to understanding Balzac's correspondence with women.

III

In *Sauf le nom,* Jacques Derrida discusses the act of naming, renaming, and nicknaming in the following terms:

> The name: What does one call thus? What does one understand under the name of name? And what occurs when one gives a name? What does one give then? [...] What happens, above all, when it is necessary to sur-name, renaming there where, precisely, the name comes to be found lacking? What makes the proper name into a sort of sur-name, pseudonym, or cryptonym at once singular and singularly untranslatable?[59]

Balzac's letters show a clear fondness for renaming, 'where, precisely, the name comes to be found lacking'. His penchant for naming and renaming his female correspondents can be viewed in terms of a nostalgia or longing for the original figure of the mother. Balzac had a liking for certain female names, which he uses only for selected female correspondents. The names Laure and Marie were particularly dear to him. Writing to Madame de Berny in March 1822, he revels in the fact that he had been granted permission to call her Laure, stressing the fact that 'Laure est un nom chéri pour moi' [The name Laure is very dear to me] (*Corr,* I, 102).[60] She was called Louise Antoinette Laure de Berny, and to everyone else she went by the name Antoinette; only Balzac called her Laure. (In *Le Lys dans la vallée,* Balzac depicts a similar dynamic: Madame de Mortsauf allows Félix to call her Henriette, which was the name used by her favourite aunt; her husband calls her Blanche.) As we have seen, the name Laure was that of Balzac's mother — and sister. Being permitted to call Madame de Berny by the name Laure thus creates links with these earlier, maternal, figures from Balzac's life.

To several other correspondents, Balzac gave the name Marie — namely to the marquise de Castries, the duchesse d'Abrantès, and to Hélène de Valette. His lovers apparently did not object; the marquise de Castries went so far as to plead with Balzac on one occasion in 1834 to continue to call her Marie — 'je suis votre amie, votre Marie' [I am your friend, your Marie] — after he rather coolly addressed her in a letter as 'Madame' (*Corr,* I, 1009). Editors of the *Correspondance* have pointed out the interesting fact that the first name of the duchesse d'Abrantès was in fact Laure, and that Marie did not figure amongst her names (see *Corr,* I, 1236, n. 2). Balzac's decision to call her Marie, therefore, suggests that the name Laure had a very special significance indeed, being attributable only to his mother, his sister, and his first lover, all three highly important figures. Yet despite this apparent need to differentiate between these two names, what they both have in common is that both are linked to maternal figures; Laure to the real-life mother, and Marie to the archetypal biblical mother figure. Baron points out that this preoccupation with the biblical mother figure Marie is visible in *La Comédie humaine*.[61] Marie and Laure also evoke archetypal lovers and muses, being the preferred female names of several of Balzac's literary icons; Laura was Petrarch's fleeting muse, and Marie (or Maria in the original English text) was evoked in Laurence Sterne's *A Sentimental Journey* (1768) — a work which, like *Tristram Shandy,* was much admired by Balzac.[62] To be able to write to a Laure and a Marie is to situate himself in a long line of great literary figures whose ranks he wishes to join.[63] Linking the figures of the mother and the lover, Balzac is also modelling himself on his literary icons. This preoccupation with naming potential lovers either Laure or Marie can be explained, as Uwe Vogel suggests, as being part of a search for the 'ideal' woman, with Balzac attempting to fashion each new lover into a preconceived 'type'; however, it also points to a central preoccupation with the fundamental lack in Balzac's life — that of a maternal figure, which his correspondence tries to fill.[64]

This becomes even more apparent if we consider how the name Ève fits into this pattern. Shortly after Éveline Hanska arrives on the scene, she is rechristened 'Ève', which may at first glance appear to be a deviation from Balzac's patterns of naming, a departure from all the Maries and Laures; it is also quite recognizably an abbreviation of her own name, supporting Balzac's claim that the relationship with Éveline was original, unique, and signalled a new beginning. When he asked Madame Hanska's permission to call her Ève, Balzac stated that this name was to represent the fact that she was the only woman in the world for him.[65] As Baron notes, Madame Hanska's abbreviated name evokes 'le premier homme rencontrant la mère de l'humanité et recommençant l'histoire du monde' [the first man meeting the mother of all humanity, and recommencing the history of the world from scratch]; indeed, this is how Balzac describes his early relationship with Madame Hanska, and his renaming of her is symbolic of this new beginning.[66]

In his first letter to the *Étrangère,* Balzac addressed her only as 'Madame'.[67] It appears that she initially disclosed her first name to Balzac as 'Évelina', for this is what he called her the first time there was an explicit mention of her name in the correspondence.[68] Balzac's first mention of 'Ève' and his reference to the blank page are both made in the same letter, dated 9 September 1833; thus both the name and the page come to symbolize new beginnings:

> Comment ne voulez-vous pas que je vous aime, vous la première, qui soyez venue à travers les espaces réchauffer un cœur qui désespérait de l'amour. [...] Eh bien, ma chère Ève, laissez-moi abréger votre nom, il vous dira mieux ainsi que vous êtes tout le sexe pour moi, la seule femme qu'il y ait dans le monde, vous le remplissez à vous seule, comme la première femme pour le premier homme. [69]

> [How do you expect me not to love you, you, the first one to ever come to me, travelling across distances to warm a heart that was despairing of love. [...] Well, my dear Eve, let me shorten your name, it will tell you all the better that you are the entire sex for me, the only woman there is in the world, you fill it all by yourself, like the first woman did for the first man.]

The insistence here is really on the idea of her as the 'first woman' in his life; the desire to refer to her as 'Ève' seems to spring quite organically from this notion borrowed from the story of Genesis. Though he tries to represent himself as the 'first man', Balzac's insistence on the biblical connotations of the name essentially reinforces his status as creator: the biblical Eve, being one of the earliest 'characters' of the human race, embodies the concept of creation. The undertone of the biblical story of creation is present in the correspondence from the beginning, if we consider how Balzac's first letter to her used the imagery of dispersed molecules (an image akin to biblical chaos) and alluded to an original language which only the two correspondents understand ('in the beginning was the Word').

Though Eve's actions are generally perceived in the same light as Pandora's — as having 'let loose evil in the world' — they in fact represent the acquisition of knowledge.[70] It is from the tree of knowledge that Eve plucked the forbidden fruit; it is knowledge, and self-awareness, that she and Adam gained upon eating from the tree. Eve's gesture is a gift to humankind rather than a misstep; her actions are at the root of all curiosity, and therefore of scholarship, learning, and creative freedom. Paul Ricœur suggests that, when she was offered access to a limitless knowledge, her story became not just about 'the desire for infinity', but also 'the infinity of desire itself; [...] the desire of desire, taking possession of knowing, of willing, of doing and of being'.[71] The concept of the insatiability of desire thus sits at the heart of the biblical story. Unsurprisingly, Eve has also come to be associated with the 'forbidden fruit' of sexual desire — even though it was not in fact sexuality or lust which in the biblical story precipitated the fall of man. Being a Catholic, Balzac was undoubtedly mindful of the name's inevitable connotations with 'sin'.

There is clearly a sexual tension at play in the naming of Madame Hanska as 'Ève'. The renaming marks a transition in the tone of the letters, from understated and respectful, to more exalted and lustful. In Balzac's *La Comédie humaine*, the name Ève is directly linked to adultery (the adulterous Béatrix is compared to Eve; another example is the novel *Une fille d'Ève*, which portrays a tempted young wife). In Balzac's letters to Madame Hanska, the name Ève is arguably used in more sexualized contexts than the name Éva. Perhaps Ève had stronger, more unambiguous connotations than it does today, evoking, as it does, the fall of man, original sin, the forbidden fruit, and the serpent. It would seem that to call a nineteenth-century lover 'mon Ève' [my Eve] as opposed to 'mon Éva' would have knowingly introduced these sexual connotations.

We can find evidence of this by looking at the occurrences of the two names in the letters. According to Kiriu's concordance, the name Éva occurs 46 times, and Ève occurs on 198 occasions.[72] A comparison of the two lists reveals that the comments made by Balzac to his 'Ève' are generally of a more salacious nature than those made to his 'Éva', which tend to be tame and respectful, very much in line with 'courtly' expressions of love. It is no accident that Balzac used the name Ève more frequently in the later years of the correspondence, by which time the relationship had become more familiar, and the vocabulary of the letters ever so slightly more telling of the sexual nature of their relationship. To give just a few examples: '[m]a grosse bonne tendre et voluptueuse Ève' [my plump, good, tender, and voluptuous Eve]; 'cette damnée maison, où nous ferons un paradis avec Ève et beaucoup de pommes' [this damned house where we will make ourselves a paradise with Eve and plenty of apples]; '[e]ncore mille baisers à mon Ève, la mille fois caressée et désirée' [a thousand more kisses to my Eve, who is caressed and desired a thousand times over]; and, perhaps most telling of all, 'je fais pour mon Ève toutes les folies qu'un Hulot fait pour une Marneffe' [for my Eve, I commit all the follies of a Hulot for his Marneffe].[73] In thus comparing 'his Ève' to Madame Marneffe — the beautiful, insatiable courtesan in *La Cousine Bette,* who brings men to their ruin through her expensive tastes — Balzac invests the name Ève with connotations of mistress, voluptuous lover, and, in a sense, 'fallen woman'. It is significant that, in the first letter in which he names Madame Hanska 'Ève', Balzac almost immediately reverts to the name Éva, perhaps sensing that he had overstepped the mark.

This act of renaming has a further significance if we consider that names have cultural resonances, and that they reflect the cultural landscape and 'linguistic convention' of their wearer (and namer).[74] The name Évelina (by which Madame Hanska would appear to have introduced herself) contains clear resonances of the linguistic landscape of the country into which Madame Hanska was born (the feminine ending 'a' is common to all Polish female first names, and is a central feature of Polish grammar).[75] Given that the name Évelina is more instantly recognizable as Polish, while the name Ève contains no trace of Polish origin, in his first act of naming her, Balzac is not only modifying her name to one which has the connotations discussed above, but he is also essentially effacing its cultural resonances. If Évelina evokes otherness, then in altering her name Balzac renders his correspondent more familiar to him, or turns her into a sort of 'everywoman' figure — all the better to be invested with new meanings of Balzac's choosing.

If we consider that Balzac was himself trying to break free from his origins, the act of effacing his correspondent's past had only positive connotations for him and for their potential future relationship. In symbolically altering her legal name — the name which would figure on her marriage certificate, for instance — Balzac invited her to let go of her past self and enter into a new identity, one which would make a relationship with him possible. In the light of this, the reference to 'naissance' [birth] in the following comment by Balzac, 'je pense aux rares perfections de celle qui fut à sa naissance la bien nommée Ève, car elle est seule sur la terre, il n'y a pas deux anges semblables' [I think of the rare perfections of the one who at birth was aptly named Eve, for she is the only one on earth, there are no two angels alike], can be seen as a reference to her 're-birth' as the Ève whom he has created.[76]

Yet, contrary to this seductive rhetoric of the 'first woman', 'Ève' Hanska was not, in fact, Balzac's first Eve; and she does have her place in Balzac's pattern of renaming women and reusing names — a fact which it is possible to spot if we read the *Lettres à Madame Hanska* together with the rest of Balzac's correspondence. While Madame Hanska is the only woman whom Balzac's letters address as 'Ève,' what Balzac's readers have generally missed is that there was in fact another Ève hidden amongst his correspondents.

In her early letters to Balzac, on four occasions, Balzac's first lover Madame de Berny signed off her letters by referring to herself as his 'Ève': 'Je te baise partout.

Je suis toute à toi, toute ton Ève' [I kiss you all over. I am wholly yours, wholly your Eve] (*Corr*, I, 554); 'Mon doux Seigneur veut-il prendre toutes les caresses que dépose ici pour lui son Ève aimante' [Would my sweet Lord accept all the caresses which are left here for him by his loving Eve] (*Corr*, I, 569); 'Ah! mon René quel arrêt pour ta nouvelle Ève' [Ah! My René, what an order for your new Eve] (*Corr*, I, 603); 'Oh! mon sublime poète, mon Seigneur, mon ange, ton Ève en ce moment est digne de ton chaste et adorable amour. Viens, viens!' [Oh! my sublime poet, my Lord, my angel, your Eve is right at this moment worthy of your chaste and adorable love. Come, come!] (*Corr*, I, 795). This 'Ève' has so far escaped the attention of critics interested in Balzac's correspondence with Madame Hanska (this reference goes unnoticed in Vogel's analysis of Balzac's naming patterns, nor does it appear in the *Concordance* by Kazuo Kiriu). Yet it is crucial to consider 'Ève' Hanska and 'Ève' de Berny together. The idea of 'Ève' Hanska as the first woman is now turned on its head. It is not just that Madame de Berny, and not Madame Hanska, was Balzac's first lover; his claim that by calling Madame Hanska 'Ève' he is granting her the status of his 'première femme' [first woman] is completely undermined by the fact that this symbolic name had already been granted to another. When, for example, Balzac writes 'Tu es et le commencement et la fin, ma chérie, mon Ève, comprend donc l'Ève, je suis aussi exclusif que tu peux l'être' [You are both the beginning and the end, my darling, my Eve, please understand, Eve, that I am as exclusive as you yourself might be], our interpretation of the romantic content of these words is necessarily influenced by this knowledge.[77] Madame Hanska is 'le commencement' only insofar as she is a redrafting of the original figure of the mother, a new embodiment of both Madame Balzac and Madame de Berny. The 'première femme', whom Balzac wishes to make into the 'avant-première femme' [*first* first woman] is in fact always a '*seconde*-première femme' [second first woman], an attempt at a new draft, but one which contains clear traces of the original.[78]

Did Balzac *give* the name 'Ève' to his first lover? We do not have the entire correspondence of Balzac and Madame de Berny, whose collection of letters from Balzac was burnt at her own request after her death; and therefore it is not possible to say when she first began using this name, nor do we know whether she chose it herself. It would seem highly likely that the suggestion was Balzac's, or at least that it was an idea that Balzac seized upon and attempted to direct to his own ends. The phrase '*your* Ève' is somewhat telling; in another letter, Madame de Berny describes herself as 'une chérie *façonnée à ton usage*' [a darling *fashioned for your use*] (*Corr*, I, 570, my emphasis); certainly, Balzac seems to be 'fashioning' his lovers as he sees fit. All we do know for sure is that, on four occasions in the few letters of hers that remain, the name 'Ève' figures in Madame de Berny's love letters to Balzac.

In the first of Madame de Berny's sign-offs quoted above ('Je te baise partout. Je suis toute à toi, toute ton Ève'), her words link the act of naming to possession — like the marquise de Castries reclaiming her right to remain his 'Marie', Madame de Berny is reinforcing her position as his 'Eve', in the face of a possible rejection — and also fairly explicitly to sexuality. This is her first mention of herself as Balzac's Ève in the *Correspondance*, where she apparently negates her own identity at her own instigation. Madame de Berny seems to enter willingly into a game which also has an element of distancing at its core; in the second sign-off, in referring to herself and Balzac in the third person, the correspondent enters into the spirit of playing a role, a theme which (at Balzac's instigation) runs through his correspondence with Madame Hanska. This willingness of de Berny to take on a different role can be seen as playful and embracing of transgression, but also perhaps as dangerous, insofar as she facilitates Balzac's apparent fantasy of not writing to a real person.

With regard to the sign-off apparently comparing him to Chateaubriand's Romantic hero 'René', Madame de Berny's fearsome 'arrêt' [order] was to help Balzac correct *Louis Lambert*. (Notably, the very next letter in the published collection, dating from July or August 1832, is a fictional love letter from this novel, sent by Balzac to the marquise de Castries; it is not unlikely that one lover helped correct writing which was then sent out with the aim of seducing the next.) It is not entirely clear why de Berny should refer to herself as Balzac's 'nouvelle Ève' [new Eve].[79] It is likely to be an echo of Rousseau's *La Nouvelle Héloïse*, and therefore both a reference to letter-writing and to the fictionalization of their relationship, setting it firmly in the realm of Romantic imaginings. This kind of fictionalization, this tendency for the boundaries between fictions and the 'reality' of the relationship to become blurred, is another characteristic that recurs in Balzac's correspondence with Madame Hanska.

Perhaps Madame de Berny considered herself a 'better version' of the biblical Eve. There was a first Eve, and now Laure de Berny is taking her place. There was also a first 'Lord', and now there is Balzac. The religious vocabulary of these letters substantiates this suggestion — 'mon Seigneur' [my Lord], 'chaste', 'sublime' — and even apparently innocuous terms of affection such as 'mon ange' [my angel] here have a biblical, metaphysical quality. In the final sign-off, in which she refers to Balzac both as 'mon [...] poète' [my [...] poet] and 'mon Seigneur' [my Lord] — with a capital letter — Madame de Berny draws attention to Balzac's privileged status of creator. The letters from 'Ève' highlight the process of creation and creativity which is at the centre of this activity of naming and renaming.

I have dwelt at some length on these sign-offs from the letters of Madame de Berny in order to reinforce the idea that, in the relationship with Madame Hanska, Balzac is frequently to be found effacing or hiding his sources and origins. To Madame Hanska, he claims to have no past, no mother, no other lovers, to have been born anew; but in fact he is just reusing old ideas and tropes that have proven their worth in previous relationships. The use of the name Ève is a case in point, and Madame de Berny would surely have been devastated to learn that this intimate element of their communication was transported, more or less wholesale in terms of the details, into a new correspondence with a younger woman.

Each of Balzac's three favourite female names — Laure, Marie, Ève — represents a mother figure: Laure the mother of Balzac; Marie the mother of Christ; Ève the mother of all humankind (and also a much more sexualized figure than the others). These names interweave in unexpected ways; for example, as we have seen, Laure (de Berny) is also an Ève; the duchesse d'Abrantès, real name Laure, is nicknamed by Balzac 'Marie.' For Balzac, these three names become the embodiment of certain concepts and he thus frequently 'rechristens' the women he meets accordingly. The point to stress is that when Éveline Hanska appears in Balzac's life, she becomes embedded in this system of pre-existing meanings in his mind; while in terms of her appearance and character she appears to Balzac as a 'blank page', her name will have brought to his mind various ideas and images which subsequently resurface in their correspondence.

If we now consider the correspondence with Éveline in the light of Balzac's earlier correspondence with the marquise de Castries, here too we begin to notice echoes that make certain letters to Madame Hanska sound like palimpsestuous rewritings of letters to de Castries. More interesting still is the fact that both relationships began under strikingly similar circumstances: both women wrote anonymous letters to him after reading *La Peau de chagrin*, expressing their opinions on his work; both were highly desirable to Balzac, not least on account of their nobility and wealth.

On 5 October 1831, Balzac replied to a letter from an unknown woman, or *Inconnue*, as Balzac termed her.[80] This was the marquise de Castries. Balzac's ensuing flirtation with the wealthy marquise came to a head in October 1832 when they met in Geneva, where Balzac made a passionate declaration of his feelings to her and was rejected. The affair with the *Inconnue* thus ended up being a blow to Balzac's ego, the shattering of a fantasy, and a considerable drain on his time and finances, as he followed her around various fashionable cities, spending money excessively to impress her. The marquise was also famously still in love with her former lover Metternich, and she was insulted that Balzac did not understand the depth of her passion for this man. It is likely the marquise cited not only her lack of romantic interest in him, but also his inferior social status, as her reasons for rejecting him.[81]

Balzac had taken up the correspondence with de Castries in October 1831, and that with Hanska began in February 1832.[82] From May to October 1832 (the date of Balzac's humiliating rejection by the marquise) the two exchanges of seductive letters overlap. Writing to two potential lovers simultaneously, Balzac was, as Robb points out, 'insuring himself against defeat'.[83] The correspondence with Madame Hanska (a second *Inconnue*) was an opportunity to rewrite his life and himself, and to avoid earlier mistakes. When the humiliation with de Castries took place, with Balzac embarrassing himself with his misjudged declarations of love, the letters to Madame Hanska became a way to protect his ego from being shattered; for in *this* correspondence at least Balzac could pretend that he had never known failure.[84] The writing of parallel correspondences becomes an act of reparation. By taking on multiple correspondences, Balzac protected himself from the failures of a Félix de Vandenesse.

The extent to which the correspondence with Madame Hanska draws on that with de Castries is striking. In comparing Balzac's letters to the two women, we again find evidence against his claim that the epistolary love affair with Madame Hanska was his 'first', or that it was authentic and original. In 1835, for instance, Balzac sends both Madame Hanska and the marquise de Castries similar letters hinting that each woman has served as a model for the sublime heroine of *Le Lys dans la vallée*. Balzac writes to Madame Hanska: 'je prépare une grande et belle œuvre, intitulée *Le Lys dans la vallée,* une figure de femme charmante, pleine de cœur, ayant un mari maussade, et vertueuse' [I am preparing a great and beautiful work, entitled *Le Lys dans la vallée,* a charming female figure, full of heart, with a gloomy husband, and virtuous].[85] The marquise de Castries received a similar letter around the same time, which speaks of 'la grande figure de femme' [the great figure of a woman] and an 'image de la perfection sur la terre' [image of perfection on earth].[86]

Comparing Balzac's first letter to the Marquise de Castries with the first letter he sent to Madame Hanska, one finds that both contain similar ideas and express them in phrases which are clear echoes of one another, as both involve Balzac writing to an unknown woman. To de Castries, he writes: 'Vous m'avez, malheureusement placé dans *la triste nécessité de parler de moi,* et c'est une grande faute en s'adressant à une femme dont je ne sais ni l'âge, ni la situation' [You have unfortunately forced me into the *sad necessity of talking about myself,* and that is a great fault when addressing a woman whose age and situation I do not know] (*Corr,* I, 409, my emphasis). To Madame Hanska, he writes a very similar letter: 'Mon chagrin est de ne pouvoir vous parler de vous que comme d'une espérance, d'un rêve du ciel, de tout ce qui est beau, — *je ne puis donc vous parler que de moi*' [I am sad to be unable to speak of you other than as a sort of hope, as a heavenly dream, as everything that is beautiful, — *therefore I can only talk to you about myself*].[87] The two letters are as though two drafts, traces of the first still visible underneath the second; and each letter, a preoccupation with writing the 'moi' [self] takes centre stage.

Nor are the 'rêveries [...] ravissantes' [ravishing reveries] of Balzac's letters to Madame Hanska safe from being 'plagiarized' in this way in his later correspondence with other women.[88] In his first letter to Madame Hanska, cited at the start of this chapter, Balzac evoked the image of a fulgurant world which connects the two of them:

> Si quelque étoile a jailli de votre bougie, si votre oreille vous a redit des murmures inconnus, si vous avez vu des figures dans le feu, si quelque chose a pétillé, a parlé près de vous, autour de vous, croyez que mon esprit errait sous vos lambris.[89]

> [If ever some spark flared from your candle, if your ear has repeated to you some unknown murmur, if you have seen a silhouette in the fire, if you heard something crackle, something speak close to you, please believe that it was my spirit roaming about under your wainscoting.]

This Romantic imagery, where flashes from the candle or the fireplace are to transmit to Madame Hanska Balzac's thoughts of her, recurs two months later in a letter to Delphine de Girardin, or, as Balzac here addresses her, '*Delphine divine*' [*divine Delphine*] (*Corr,* I, 603), in which he clearly 'recycles' a sentence: 'Avez-vous pensé que je pensais à vous [...]? Quand la bougie a scintillé, quand votre oreille a résonné, quand vous avez été gaie, avez-vous cru que j'étais près de vous en esprit?' [Did you ever think that I was thinking of you [...]? When your candle twinkled, when something rang in your ear, when you were happy, did you believe that I was near you in spirit?] (*Corr,* I, 602–03).[90]

Much as it is natural to think of writers reusing their own imagery, here it is particularly striking because of Balzac's continued insistence in the correspondence to Madame Hanska of the originality, authenticity, and uniqueness of their relationship and his feelings towards it.

'Recycling' names and Romantic imagery is of course exploited in novels, as well as letters. Madame Hanska's name, so symbolic of the creation of something new — and yet also, paradoxically, evoking a return to the familiar — comes to play a role in Balzac's fiction in ways which allow him to explore and exploit all these associations.

While the correspondence with Madame Hanska was in the early stages, Balzac informed her that he had named two of his characters after her. One of these was Ève Séchard in *Illusions perdues* (1837–43). This character was expressly created as a tribute to Madame Hanska, but only after she and Balzac had already met and fallen in love. 'Dans *Illusions perdues,* il y a une jeune fille nommée *Ève* qui est à mes yeux la plus ravissante création que j'aurai faite' [In *Illusions perdues,* there is a young woman named *Ève* who is, to my eyes, the most ravishing creature I will ever have made], Balzac wrote in December 1836.[91] Ève's role in *Illusions perdues,* and the (mostly positive) biblical associations of her name, have been well summarized by Baron: Ève Séchard, an Ève before the Fall, is the perfect partner and sister.[92] Much as Balzac ostensibly attributes positive qualities to Madame Hanska when he refers to her as 'Ève', he likewise attributes positive characteristics to this fictional namesake.

The other — less discussed, and, I would argue, more important — tribute to Madame Hanska is Évelina in *Le Médecin de campagne,* a character created soon after Balzac learned her real name.[93] *Le Médecin de campagne* was begun in September 1832 and finished in the summer of 1833, and was originally intended to contain a thinly veiled account of Balzac's rejection by the marquise de Castries.[94] In the end, Balzac simply inserted the Évelina character in place of the one based on de Castries, replacing this haughty and ruthless persona with the pure and virtuous Évelina (and we know by now how readily Balzac finds women 'replaceable').

On 19 July 1833, Balzac wrote to Hanska, telling her of his delight at her imagined reaction to this novel: 'Elle frémira de joie, en voyant que *son nom* m'a occupé, qu'elle était présente à ma pensée, et que ce que je pensais de plus beau, de plus noble, de la jeune fille j'en ai chargé *son nom.* Vous verrez en lisant ce livre que vous étiez dans mon âme comme la lumière' [She will tremble with joy to see that *her name* was on my mind, that she was present in my thoughts, and that I made *her name* stand for all the most beautiful, the most noble thoughts that I had of this young girl. You will see when you read this book that you were in my soul like a light].[95] In August, he tells her 'vous verrez un nom tracé avec bonheur sur chaque page' [you will see a name traced with joy on every page].[96] On 9 September 1833, he asks for her reaction: 'Vous avez lu maintenant *Le Médecin.* [...] Avez-vous posé le livre au moment où Benassis laisse échapper le nom adoré?' [You have now read *Le Médecin.* [...] Did you put the book down at the point when Benassis lets slip the beloved name?][97]

This repeated insistence on the name — 'son nom', 'le nom adoré' — is important in understanding the significance of the Évelina story, in which a character was based on a name, and the real person behind it was unknown. Similarly to the real-life 'Évelina', whose perfections Balzac could only imagine, the 'Évelina' in the novel is a blank slate, which the narrator-storyteller attempts to fill as best he can.

Évelina is the woman loved by the male narrator, the doctor Benassis, of *Le Médecin de campagne*. Against the strangely alluring backdrop of her parents' silent and monastic household (which is represented as something of a 'blank page' itself), the narrator begins to fall in love with the girl, and thinks he can likewise detect in her the symptoms of a first love. He omits to tell her, or her parents, that he has had a previous relationship, which resulted in the birth of a child out of wedlock. When this is discovered, Évelina is banned from seeing him. With her mother's permission, she writes him a letter (the only direct communication he ever receives from her) to say a gracious and reserved goodbye — and also, curiously, to ask him to entrust his child to her, should he ever find himself in need. Benassis reacts angrily to her letter, seeing it only as a rejection. He spends the rest of his life regretting his harsh reply, jumping eagerly at the chance to narrate the story of this unrequited love to a willing listener.

Balzac scholars have been left mostly underwhelmed by Balzac's puritanical representation of Évelina, and have consequently dismissed her as pale and uninteresting. Baron describes her as 'une jeune femme idéale mais un peu fade' [an ideal yet rather bland young woman];[98] Bernard Guyon, in his study of the Évelina episode, mentions only her pale face which, in his view, fails to arrest our attention;[99] and Herbert Hunt expresses surprise that such an overly virtuous character was ever given leave to exist.[100] Critical studies have mostly ignored Évelina; even the 2003 issue of the *Année balzacienne* devoted specially to rereadings of *Le Médecin de campagne* contains no study of this character. There seems to be a general view that the Évelina episode is an addition which is not crucial to the general plot of the novel.

I would like to challenge this misrepresentation of Évelina as lacking in interest, and suggest that her interest lies precisely in her apparently elusive, insipid nature. What has hitherto not been appreciated is that this character is in fact a study in what the creative imagination can do when it has almost nothing to go on (in Balzac's case, a few letters and a name; in Benassis's case, silences and the occasional glance). Balzac was trying to write a tribute to the new 'Évelina' in his life; however, not knowing much about her, and fearful of taking any creative liberties which might cause her offence, he kept closely to the model he had — the real-life Évelina who was still little more than a 'blank page'. Both 'Évelinas', the fictional and the real, are chiefly constructed around a blank, an ellipsis, a silence.

In representing her thus, he places the focus on the male narrator's attempts at 'reading' her, just as he himself was attempting to 'read' Madame Hanska. Crucially, Évelina in *Le Médecin de campagne* is only ever represented through the narrator's perception of her, and is reduced to being the product of another character's guesswork (and memory). If, then, Évelina seems bland and insipid to readers, this may be because Balzac only presents her through Benassis's (mis)interpretation of her — just as his own portrayals of Éveline Hanska in his letters relied largely on imagination. Throughout the story, the character is mostly represented as silent, with very little of her speech reported back, and the narrator imagines that she is trying to communicate with him in a non-verbal way. 'Elle me remercia par un regard doux, presque humide. Nous nous étions tout dit' [She thanked me by a soft, almost humid look. We had thus told each other everything], the narrator says on one occasion (*CH*, IX, 562). Yet Balzac hints that her quiet demeanour is not necessarily being interpreted correctly. We might question, for example, the narrator's selective reporting of Évelina's words; Évelina is not entirely silent, yet most of her words are not recorded. The narrator makes reference to interpreting the 'modulations de sa voix pour y *chercher* ses plus secrètes pensées' [modulations of her voice, *searching them* for her innermost thoughts] (*CH*, IX, 561, my emphasis); interestingly, he is focusing on the sound of her voice rather than ascribing value to her actual words. It is as though they have been edited out, the silence being more conducive to the creation of his own narratives.

Silence plays a part in the process of falling in love; yet the narrator himself concedes that the silence of Évelina's home led to the smallest events becoming overblown. 'Pour un homme aussi sincèrement épris que je l'étais, le silence, la simplicité de la vie [...] donnèrent plus de force à l'amour. Par ce calme profond, les moindres mouvements, une parole, un geste acquiéraient un intérêt prodigieux' [For a man as sincerely besotted as I was, the silence, the simplicity of that life [...] gave my love a greater force. In this profound calm, the smallest movements, a word, a gesture, acquired a prodigious interest] (*CH*, IX, 560). It is on the basis of the smallest gestures and fragments of knowledge that the narrator tries to judge his love object.

Balzac's Évelinas (both fictional and real) are the product of guesswork, as we see in the vocabulary of the following passage, from *Le Médecin de campagne,* where the admirer tries to attach significance to the smallest of signals and signs:

> Les moindres accidents contractèrent alors un prix excessif. L'admirer pendant des heures entières, attendre une réponse et savourer longtemps les modulations de sa voix pour y chercher ses plus secrètes pensées; épier le tremblement de ses doigts quand je lui présentais quelque objet qu'elle avait cherché, [...] tous ces riens étaient de grands événements. [...] Je finis par deviner que ce timide silence était le seul moyen qui pût servir à cette jeune fille pour exprimer ses sentiments. (*CH*, IX, 561)

> [The smallest occurrences commanded the heaviest price. To admire her for hours on end, to await a reply and to slowly savour the modulations of her voice in order to search for her most secret thoughts; to spy the tremor of her fingers when I presented her with some object she had been looking for. [...] all those nothings were grand events. [...] I ended up guessing that this timid silence was the only way this young girl had of expressing her feelings.]

In another passage, the narrator's certainty that he has interpreted Évelina's motivations correctly is called into question by the very form the extract takes. The negative, interrogative constructions — 'N'était-elle pas [...]?' [Was she not [...]?]; 'n'écoutait-elle pas [...]?' [did she not listen [...]?'] — highlight the question mark which hangs over Évelina's motivations; and the reader realizes that we cannot in fact be sure if the interpretation of Benassis is entirely correct:

N'était-elle pas toujours dans le salon quand j'y venais? n'y restait-elle pas durant ma visite attendue ou pressentie peut-être! cette fidélité silencieuse n'accusait-elle pas le secret de son âme innocente? Enfin, n'écoutait-elle pas mes discours avec un plaisir qu'elle ne savait pas cacher? (*CH*, IX, 561)

[Was she not always in the salon whenever I came? Did she not stay there throughout my visit, which she had awaited, or perhaps foreseen! Did not this silent loyalty point to the secret of her innocent soul? Finally, did she not listen to my speeches with a pleasure which she knew not how to hide?]

The one time Évelina really makes her own 'voice' heard is when, with the permission of her mother, she writes Benassis a letter to explain that, although she forgives him his faults, she can never marry him. Arguably, this letter, subjected to the mother's approval and therefore perhaps her censorship, may not fully reveal the young woman's true feelings and thoughts. Yet this is also the time when, by his own admission, Benassis chooses to interpret her words incorrectly:

Cette lettre, pleine de sentiments généreux, trompait mes espérances [...]. Aussi d'abord n'écoutai-je que ma douleur; plus tard, j'ai respiré le parfum que cette jeune fille essayait de jeter sur les plaies de mon âme en s'oubliant elle-même; mais, dans le désespoir, je lui écrivis un peu durement. (*CH*, IX, 567)

[This letter, filled with generosity, dashed my hopes [...]. Thus at first I remained deaf to anything except my own pain; some time later, I could feel the fragrance with which this young girl tried to soothe the wounds in my soul by forgetting herself; but, in my despair, I wrote back to her rather harshly.]

Évelina's letter is, arguably, the most significant communication she makes, but Benassis responds to it only as prompted by his own hurt feelings. The correspondence of Évelina and Benassis — be it only three letters — allows Balzac to comment on some of the creative, indeed delusional processes which are at stake in the interpretation of evidence, and which prevent the letter-reader from really 'reading' the other. As we have seen in the Introduction, Benassis attaches more importance to *his own* letter to Évelina than hers to him; thus he supports Balzac's statement that 'Nous nous aimons nous-mêmes en *l'autre*' [It is ourselves we love in the *other*] (*CH*, IX, 562). Benassis, who had given so much thought to interpreting Évelina's looks, gestures, silences, and insignificant words, ultimately makes the mistake of judging these according to his own projected desires. Thus in a sense she remains a 'blank page', forever to be deciphered. The fictional Évelina is vague and ungraspable just as Madame Hanska remains indefinable in the early stages of the letter-writing relationship.

Balzac's attempt at creating this fictional tribute to his Éveline is a self-reflective act, a sort of *mise en abyme* of the creative process itself (what tableau can one possibly create when there is almost nothing to go on?). The answer, which may be discomforting to Balzac, is that a fully-fledged character cannot be imagined without some concrete information; there is not much he can do with what Madame Hanska has given him at that point, at least not without tipping over into outright fantasy.

We could argue that Balzac's portrayal of Évelina in *Le Médecin de campagne* reveals to us something of what his ideal woman would be — beautiful and silent, 's'oubliant elle-même', allowing for her male admirer's interpretation to stand unchallenged. When Balzac meets Éveline in Neuchâtel in 1833, he goes from writing to an unknown and unseen correspondent to addressing an actual flesh-and-blood woman:

> Mon Éva chérie, voici donc une nouvelle vie bien délicieusement commencée pour moi. Je t'ai vue, je t'ai parlé, nos corps ont fait alliance comme nos âmes [...]. Mauvaise! tu n'as pas vu dans mes regards tout ce que je souhaitais.[101]

> [My darling Eva, a new and most delicious life has now begun for me. I have seen you, I have spoken to you, our bodies have made an alliance, as have our souls [...]. Wicked one! You did not see in my glances all that I wished you to.]

Face to face with his lover, in a sense the skilled letter-writer finds himself stripped of his greatest power: 'pourquoi me demandais-tu tant de te dire ce que je ne voulais t'exprimer que par mes regards, ces sortes d'idées perdent à la parole' [why did you keep asking me to tell you that which I only wanted to express through my gaze, those sorts of things lose meaning when put into words].[102]

As the correspondence with Éveline progresses, we see Balzac occasionally becoming disappointed whenever his correspondent fails to live up to his idealized vision of her. As early as September 1833, the letters show cracks beginning to appear in this perfect picture of his imaginary idol. In his letter of 13 September 1833, Balzac confesses to a 'peine vive' [acute pain] caused by her letter, thus writing the first of what will become a long series of letters expressing the suffering she is able to cause by her jealousy, her doubts, and her apparent incomprehension of him.[103] From now on, versions of the phrase 'Nous ne nous connaissons donc pas' [We do not know one another, then] will occasionally punctuate the correspondence like a refrain, as Balzac finds proof that the *Étrangère* possesses qualities less noble than those he imagined her to have.[104] It is one of the many ironies of Balzac's correspondence that he claims not to know her at all the better he comes to know her — in fact, of course, what is disconcerting is his realization of the ever-growing gap between fantasy and reality.

The character of Évelina reminds us of the constant tension in Balzac's letters between life and the *œuvre*, between the real and the imaginary, and, as in *Le Chef-d'œuvre inconnu*, between 'l'érotisme réel' [real eroticism] and 'l'enthousiasme esthétique' [aesthetic enthusiasm].[105] While the letters offer tangible erotic potential — the writing paper which evokes the woman's arm, the lingering scent of Madame Hanska's perfume, the small objects, such as flowers, which she inserts into her letters — they also offer, perhaps most tantalizingly, the possibility of creating her to his fancy, of giving free rein to his literary imagination.

In creating his imaginary Ève, Balzac draws on the biblical connotations of this name to evoke a persona which can be linked to the beginning of all narrative and, consequently, interpretation.[106] Balzac attempts to interpret the words, silences, and blank pages of Éveline (just as readers of Balzac's correspondence today try to interpret his readings of those missing letters in their turn). Balzac's 'Ève' is at the root of all this interpretation; she necessitates it. When Balzac creates his 'Ève', this 'creation' by no means remains a passive tableau, to be contemplated and admired by the male artist as he chooses. At the beginning of the correspondence, Balzac tries to 'write' Madame Hanska as best he can; as the correspondence unfolds, he does manage to retain control over his creation. In this pre-lapsarian stage before their first meeting, he can imagine her as he wishes; however, once they 'bite the apple', she takes on a life of her own.

Notes to Chapter 1

1. Laurence Sterne, *The Life and Opinions of Tristram Shandy, Gentleman*, ed. by Melvyn New and Joan New, 3 vols (Gainesville: University Presses of Florida, 1984), II, 566.
2. *LMH*, I, 55 (9 September 1833).
3. Anne McCall Saint-Saëns suggests that Madame Hanska's 'inspired' gesture of sending the blank page is at the heart of a game of creativity between the two correspondents. See McCall Saint-Saëns, pp. 41–50.
4. *LMH*, II, 595 (23 June 1847).
5. *LMH*, I, 418 (23 October 1837).
6. Susan Gubar, '*The Blank Page* and the Issues of Female Creativity', *Critical Inquiry*, 8 (1981), 243–63 (p. 259).
7. 'Nous aimons d'abord *un tableau*. Car il faut au coup de foudre le signe même de la soudaineté' [The first thing we love is a *tableau*. For love at first sight requires the very sign of suddenness], Roland Barthes, *Fragments d'un discours amoureux* (Paris: Seuil, 1977), p. 227.
8. I quote Diana Knight, *Balzac and the Model of Painting: Artist Stories in La Comédie humaine* (Oxford: Legenda, 2007), p. 36.
9. *LMH*, I, 55 (9 September 1833).
10. Ibid.
11. See Naomi Segal, 'To Love and Be Loved: Sartre, Anzieu and Theories of the Caress', in *Paragraph,* 32 (July 2009), 226–39.
12. *LMH*, I, 25 (end of January 1833).
13. Jean-Paul Sartre, *L'Être et le Néant* (Paris: Gallimard, 1943), p. 430.
14. Ovid, *Metamorphoses,* ed. by Madeleine Forey, trans. by Arthur Golding (London: Penguin, 2002), pp. 302–04.
15. See Knight, *Balzac and the Model of Painting*, and Alexandra Wettlaufer, *Pen vs. Paintbrush: Girodet, Balzac and the Myth of Pygmalion in Postrevolutionary France* (New York: Palgrave, 2001). See also Françoise Pitt-Rivers, *Balzac et l'art* (Paris: Chêne, 1993), and Georges Didi-Huberman, *La Peinture incarnée* (Paris: Minuit, 1985).
16. *LMH*, I, 7 (May 1832).
17. Knight draws attention to this prominent metaphor of dressing and undressing in the Pygmalion stories, *Balzac and the Model of Painting*, especially pp. 20 & 82.
18. *LMH*, I, 54 (9 September 1833).
19. *LMH*, I, 25 (end of January 1833).
20. *LMH*, I, 24 (end of January 1833).
21. There is also a resonance with *Le Chef-d'œuvre inconnu,* where Frenhofer's visitors find themselves walking *around* the canvas in order to try and comprehend it (*CH*, x, 436). Balzac's evocation of the *Étrangère* is similarly a three-dimensional experience.
22. *LMH*, I, 28 (24 February 1833).
23. *LMH*, I, 419 (7 November 1837).
24. *LMH*, I, 7 (May 1832).
25. *LMH*, I, 7 (May 1832).
26. Théophile Gautier alludes to elective affinities in *Mademoiselle de Maupin* (1835), and again in the poem 'Affinités secrètes' (1849), in *Émaux et camées* (Paris: Les Maîtres du livre, 1913), p. 7. See also *CH*, x, 1642, n. 6, and *CH*, x, 720.
27. See Gustave Flaubert, *Madame Bovary* (Paris: Librairie Gruend, 1857), p. 136.
28. Balzac himself describes his early reveries of the *Inconnue* as an 'épisode tout romanesque' (entirely novelistic episode') in this same letter (p. 8).
29. See *CH*, x, 47–55 (especially pp. 47–48 & 50). Balzac writes that while some writers do pour

their character into their works, 'il est d'autres écrivains dont l'âme et les moeurs contrastent puissamment avec la forme et le fond de leurs ouvrages' [there are other writers whose spirit and morals are in stark contrast to the style and content of their works] (p. 47). He complains of being vilified because of *La Physiologie du mariage* (1829), his philosophical work on marriage and a form of ludic self-help manual for husbands (p. 49).

30. *LMH*, I, 584 (2 June 1842).

31. The first novel Balzac published under his own name was *Le Dernier Chouan* (1829). See the story of the death of Horace de Saint-Aubin, in the 'Préface' to *La Dernière Fée ou la nouvelle lampe merveilleuse*, in Honoré de Balzac, *Premiers romans*, ed. by André Lorant, 2 vols (Paris: Laffont, Bouquins, 1999) (hereafter *PR*), I, 1063–115 (pp. 1094–95). It was actually Balzac's friend Félix Davin who penned this text; yet it is widely acknowledged that he wrote Balzac's prefaces very much under the latter's directives.

32. See Robb, p. 4: 'His father had been born a Balssa. It was and still is a common name in various forms in the mountains of the Auvergne — the name of a highland peasant; and so, as he rose through the ranks of society, he changed it to the name of an ancient noble family, eventually adding the supposedly aristocratic "de"'. Pierre Citron notes in his 'Introduction' to *El Verdugo* (1829) that 'pour la première fois l'écrivain signe une œuvre "H. de Balzac", utilisant cette particule que Bernard-François s'était indûment attribuée dans certains faire-part de mariage de sa fille Laurence' (*CH*, X, 1129). On the origins of the name Balssa, see Jean-Louis Déga, *La Vie prodigieuse de Bernard-François Balssa: aux sources historiques de "La Comédie humaine"* (Rodez: Subervie, 1998), pp. 13–15.

33. See *LMH*, I, 16 (7 November & 9 December 1832). For a discussion of representations of the father figure in Balzac's fictions of the late 1820s and the connection between Balzac's father and the way in which Balzac signed his works, see Robb, pp. 161–62.

34. Although a more usual term to use here would be 'palimpsestic', I have chosen the word 'palimp*sestuous*', with its connotation of sexuality, in order to foreground the wider implications of Balzac's 'layered' writing; I wish to make more explicit the link between Balzac's palimpsestic writing and the way this writing points to how his many relationships with women ultimately connect.

35. *LMH*, II, 503 (1 January 1847).

36. *LMH*, I, 625 (20 December 1842).

37. Laure Surville, *Balzac, sa vie et ses œuvres d'après sa correspondance* (Paris: Librairie Nouvelle, 1858), p. 3.

38. 'Devenu maigre et chétif, Honoré ressemblait à ces somnambules qui dorment les yeux ouverts, il n'entendait pas la plupart des questions qu'on lui adressait et ne savait que répondre' [Skinny and sickly, Honoré was like those sleepwalkers who sleep with their eyes open, he did not hear most of the questions he was asked and did not know how to reply] (Surville, pp. 20–21).

39. Surville, p. 5.

40. The 'alcôve' was a dark cupboard where the boys were locked up as a punishment.

41. *LMH*, II, 270 (23 July 1846). This marriage plan resulted from Madame Hanska's unexpected pregnancy; following her miscarriage, the marriage was postponed.

42. *LMH*, II, 272 (25 July 1846).

43. *LMH*, I, 625 (20 December 1842).

44. *LMH*, I, 608 (17 October 1842).

45. *LMH*, I, 467 (15 October 1838).

46. *LMH*, I, 607 (17 October 1842).

47. Honoré de Balzac, *Pensées, sujets, fragments* (Paris: Blaizot, 1910), p. 39.

48. See Baron, *Hiéroglyphes*, p. 101.

49. Robb writes of the early relationship between Balzac and his mother that '[h]is mother had convinced him of his own defects and of the impossibility of ever pleasing her' (p. 24).

50. *LMH*, I, 599 (25 August 1842).

51. See for example Balzac's letters between January and February 1842 (*LMH*, I, 545–56), which receive no reply.

52. Sigmund Freud, 'Beyond the Pleasure Principle', in *The Standard Edition of the Complete Psychological Works,* ed. and trans. by James Strachey, 24 vols (London: Hogarth Press, 1953–74), XVIII (1961), 7–64 (p. 36).

53. See Janet Beizer, 'F/V: notes sur *Le Lys dans la vallée*', in *L'Érotique balzacienne*, ed. by Lucienne Frappier-Mazur and Jean-Marie Roulin (Paris: SEDES, 2001), pp. 11–22 (p. 22).

54. Julia Kristeva, *Pouvoirs de l'horreur: essai sur l'abjection* (Paris: Seuil, 1980), p. 52, cited in Beizer, p. 22.

55. See for example *LMH*, I, 327 (June 1836), and *LMH*, I, 530 (1 June 1841). See also the article 'Henry de Balzac', by Anne-Marie Bijaoui-Baron (later Anne-Marie Baron), in *L'Année balzacienne* (1979), 211–19.

56. Robb, pp. 26–27. I would add that it is by no means certain that the father played a lesser role in the naming of the children; we do know, however, that the mother was the more active and more influential of the two parents (see Surville, p. 5), and therefore Robb's assumption that she held more sway in naming her children is quite plausible.

57. *LMH*, II, 146 (2 January 1846). The full extract reads: 'J'ai donc été moi et Laurence l'objet de sa haine; elle a tué Laurence mais moi je vis' [So it was me and Laurence who were the object of her hatred; she killed Laurence but I am still alive].

58. Rose Fortassier, 'Du bon usage par le romancier Balzac des souffrances du jeune Honoré', *Imaginaire & Inconscient*, 4 (2003), 39–52 (pp. 43–45).

59. Jacques Derrida, *On the Name*, ed. by Thomas Dutoit, trans. by David Wood and others (Stanford, CA: Stanford University Press, 1995). This quotation is printed on the first page of a four-page unbound insert entitled *Please Insert (Prière d'insérer)* and included with his books *Passions, Sauf le nom*, and *Khôra*.

60. This letter makes clear that de Berny is 'une autre Laure' [another Laure], coming second, in a way, to his sister (*Corr*, I, 103).

61. Anne-Marie Baron, *Balzac et la bible: une herméneutique du romanesque* (Paris: Honoré Champion, 2007), p. 168.

62. For Balzac's comments on Sterne's 'Marie' (significantly, made to Madame de Berny during his attempts to seduce her), see *Corr*, I, 115 (April 1822); see also *Corr*, I, 1214 (notes to letter 22–22), n. 1.

63. He alludes to this in a letter to Madame Hanska in 1835: 'Une femme est beaucoup dans notre vie, quand elle est Béatrix et Laure et mieux encore' [A woman counts for a lot in our lives, when she is Beatrice and Laura and more besides] (*LMH*, I, 228, 26 January 1835).

64. Vogel, pp. 40–41.

65. See for example *LMH*, I, 53 (9 September 1833).

66. Baron, *Hiéroglyphes*, p. 124.

67. *LMH*, I, 7 (May 1832).

68. *LMH*, I, 52 (end of August 1833).

69. *LMH*, I, 53 (9 September 1833).

70. I quote Linda M. Lewis, *Germaine de Staël, George Sand, and the Victorian Woman Artist* (Columbia & London: University of Missouri Press, 2003), p. 2.

71. Paul Ricœur, *The Symbolism of Evil*, trans. by Emerson Buchanan (Boston: Beacon Press, 1969), p. 253.

72. See Kazuo Kiriu, *Vocabulaire de Balzac*, <http://www.v2asp.paris.fr/commun/v2asp/musees/balzac/kiriu/lh/tome11.pdf> [accessed 11 September 2012]. I do not count the abbreviation 'E', which could arguably refer to either name, but I do include the abbreviations 'È.' and 'Èv.'.

73. *LMH*, II, 528 (19 January 1847); *LMH*, II, 496 (30 December 1846); *LMH*, II, 345 (26 September 1846); and *LMH*, II, 464 (12 December 1846).

74. This point is made by Judith Butler in *Excitable Speech: A Politics of the Performative* (New York & London: Routledge, 1997), p. 29.

75. In Polish, feminine nouns, and feminine names, take the ending 'a', and they require all relating adverbs and adjectives to follow suit. While the name 'Évelina', therefore, sounds natural in a Polish sentence, the name 'Ève' would sound dissonant.

76. *LMH*, II, 120–21 (12 December 1845).

77. *LMH*, I, 104 (1 December 1833).

78. I borrow this last phrase loosely from Daniel Sibony; it is a reference to Sibony's concept of 'le complexe du second-premier' [the complex of the second-first], see *Les Trois Monothéismes: juifs, chrétiens, musulmans entre leurs sources et leurs destins* (Paris: Seuil, 1992). Sibony discusses how people of certain faiths feel as though they came 'second' to an 'original' faith which came

before theirs. The phrase 'second-premier' aptly describes Madame Hanska's position. I am
grateful to Richard Bates for pointing out this reference.

79. See *Corr*, I, 605–06, July or August 1832.

80. See *Corr*, I, 409–12. See also Marcel Bouteron, *Études balzaciennes* (Paris: Jouve, 1954), pp.
92–118, on the story of Balzac and the marquise de Castries.

81. See Robb, pp. 213–20.

82. On 28 February 1832, *L'Étrangère* — Madame Hanska — sent her own anonymous letter to
Balzac. Balzac replied in May.

83. Robb, p. 224.

84. Robb points out that, in meeting Madame Hanska in Geneva in 1833, Balzac is able to rewrite,
as it were, what once threatened to be a bad ending as a happy one: 'Just before Christmas 1833,
Balzac set off for Geneva with the manuscript of *Eugénie Grandet* in his bag. Just over a year had
passed since he left the city in disgrace and humiliation. Now, he was referring to his second
meeting with Éveline [Madame Hanska] as the "dénoument". The rewriting of the Marquise
de Castries disaster novel was almost complete' (Robb, p. 244).

85. *LMH*, I, 235 (11 March 1835).

86. *Corr*, I, 1070–71 (letter to the marquise de Castries, dated around 10 March 1835). On the
similarity between these two letters, see Roger Pierrot, *LMH*, I, 235 (11 March 1835), n. 2.

87. *LMH*, I, 27 (24 February 1833), my emphasis.

88. *LMH*, I, 8 (May 1832).

89. *LMH*, I, 8 (May 1832). See also *LMH*, I, 282 (19 December 1835), where Balzac alludes again to
this extended metaphor.

90. Delphine de Girardin, *née* Gay, was at this point Balzac's friend and a great admirer of his novels
(she is maligned later in the correspondence). See *Corr*, I, 1553.

91. *LMH*, I, 355 (1 December 1836).

92. Anne-Marie Baron, 'L'Intertexte biblique d'*Illusions perdues*', in '*Illusions perdues*': *colloque de la
Sorbonne*, ed. by José-Luis Diaz and André Guyaux, 2nd edn (Paris: Presses de l'Université Paris-
Sorbonne, 2004), pp. 11–24 (see pp. 12–13 for Baron's study of 'Ève').

93. This novel arguably contains further tributes to Madame Hanska. See Sophie Korwin-
Piotrowska, *Balzac et le monde slave: Madame Hanska et l'œuvre balzacienne* (Paris: Librairie
Ancienne Honoré Champion, 1933), p. 160.

94. I paraphrase Herbert J. Hunt, *Balzac's Comédie humaine* (London: Athlone, 1964), p. 71. See also
Anne-Marie Baron, *Le Fils prodige: l'inconscient de La Comédie humaine* (Paris: Nathan, 1993), p. 35.

95. *LMH*, I, 44 (19 July 1833), my emphasis.

96. *LMH*, I, 52, end of August 1833.

97. *LMH*, I, 55 (9 September 1833).

98. Anne-Marie Baron, 'Fantasmes et sublimation dans *Le Médecin de campagne*', *L'Année balzacienne*
(2003), 77–90 (p. 78).

99. See Bernard Guyon, *La Création littéraire chez Balzac: la genèse du 'Médecin de campagne'*, 2nd edn
(Paris: Colin, 1969), pp. 202–33.

100. 'Of the virtuous daughter, whose part in the story is short, one thing only need to be said.
Granted that "Évelina" was conceived as a tribute to Mme Hanska, it is still surprising that
Balzac, who hated puritanism above all else, could have brought himself to invent such a
paragon of maidenly rectitude' (Hunt, p. 73).

101. *LMH*, I, 61 (6 October 1833).

102. *LMH*, I, 62 (6 October 1833). A more substantial analysis of the significance of the gaze as
it is represented in Balzac's novels and letters can be found in my article, 'An Aesthetics of
Indirection in Novels and Letters', pp. 229–46.

103. *LMH*, I, 56 (13 September 1833).

104. *LMH*, II, 85 (6 November 1833).

105. I borrow these phrases from Julia Kristeva's brief analysis of *Le Chef-d'œuvre inconnu* in *Le Génie
féminin: la vie, la folie, les mots: Hannah Arendt, Melanie Klein, Colette*, 3 vols (Paris: Fayard, 2002),
III, 491.

106. Thorell Porter-Tsomondo sees Eve as representing the origin of narrative. See *The Not So Blank
'Blank Page': The Politics of Narrative and the Woman Narrator in the Eighteenth- and Nineteenth-
Century English Novel* (New York: Peter Lang, 2007), pp. 5–6.

CHAPTER 2

❖

Performance and Play:
Balzac's Letters as Theatre

Mais quand elle se tut, sa physionomie changea, ses traits se décomposèrent, et sa figure exprima la fatigue. Elle venait d'ôter un masque; actrice, son rôle était fini.

[But when she fell silent, her physiognomy changed, her features became decomposed, and her face expressed fatigue. She had just removed a mask; the actress's role was finished.]

BALZAC, *La Peau de chagrin* (*CH*, x, 182)

L'homme est un bouffon qui danse sur des précipices!

[Man is a clown, dancing on the edge of the abyss!]

BALZAC, *La Peau de chagrin* (*CH*, x, 102)

In 1832, an anonymous female fan wrote to Balzac, setting out the writing process in the same terms as an actress might describe her preparations for a debut on the stage:

> Je cache mes cheveux noirs sous une blonde chevelure, je change mon *bibi* de Simon pour un Castor de Baudoin, je dissimule ma taille dans une redingote de Staub. Je délasse la bottine de Gélot pour chausser la botte de Fitz Patric[k] et substituant à mon nom de femme celui de Jules, je me hasarde à vous écrire. (*Corr*, I, 620)

> [I hide my black hair under a blonde wig; I exchange my Simon fascinator for a beaver fur hat from Baudoin; I conceal my waist under a Staub frock coat. I undo my little Gelot ankle shoe to put on a Fitz Patric riding boot, and substituting the name 'Jules' for my own female name, I venture to write to you.]

With a great deal of elegance, she pinpoints a key feature of letter-writing: the potential of the letter as a space for performance. Letters allow for disguises and masks; they offer the opportunity for endless self-reinvention. Just as no one performance of a play is definitive, no single letter is the definitive performance of the self, and a letter-writer is always free to adopt a new and different voice or role.

This chapter will show how Balzac uses his letters as mini-performances, to ends which of course include the seduction of Madame Hanska, but also the creation and assumption of different roles that allow him to play with his own identity. Already in the previous chapter, we saw how playing with the names of his female correspondents allows Balzac to make them to embody a myriad of characters. This process is more explicit in the letters to Madame Hanska than in any of his other correspondence. As the relationship develops and Balzac comes to know her better, he uses the correspondence to take on different roles for himself, and also to cast her opposite him in many of these. He does this for several reasons. There is a considerable element of writerly enjoyment, but there are also more practical issues at stake. As the relationship develops, it naturally becomes harder and harder for the couple to ignore the fact that Hanska is married and that any relationship between her and Balzac is therefore adulterous. Much of what Balzac does in the correspondence in terms of taking on different roles and assigning corresponding ones to Éveline is done in order to help her justify to herself the morally dubious situation that has developed between them. Balzac is essentially supplying a variety of different narratives to Hanska that allow her to explain the relationship to herself in morally defensible terms.

Balzac's wider correspondence reinforces the notion that he sees letter-writing as an opportunity for performing and donning disguises. His first letter home to his sister Laure sent from the rue Lesdiguières contains an imagined, scripted conversation between Balzac and his servant, 'Moi-Même' [Myself], complete with stage directions.[1] We remember that at the time of writing this letter Balzac had his sights set on becoming a dramatist (a project he cherished throughout his life), penning his versified tragedy *Cromwell*; the scripted conversation with 'Myself' is one instance where we see his fondness for the theatre spill over into his letter-writing. The few surviving letters to Madame de Berny likewise show a penchant for play-acting (as we saw in Chapter 1, she willingly played the part of his 'Ève', while he was her 'Lord'). In his letters to Madame de Berny, Balzac played the part of the youthful suitor, wise beyond his years; those letters show a proud young writer, determined to come across as a future great man.

By the time he is writing to Hanska, Balzac appears to have the confidence to explore a variety of roles.[2] In this correspondence, it was of course she who initiated the exchange of letters anonymously. Donning the disguise of an *Étrangère*, and insisting that Balzac would never know who she was, she instigated a dynamic of 'performance' in the sense of 'doing something "make believe", "in a play", "for fun"' (a definition of performance proposed by Richard Schechner).[3]

How Balzac 'sets the scene' for these performances, and what he achieves through them, is the focus of this chapter. If, as suggested by Schechner, the functions of performance include 'to entertain', 'to make something that is beautiful', 'to mark or change identity', 'to heal', and 'to teach, persuade, convince', Balzac's letter-writing can be said to share precisely these objectives with the act of dramatic performance.[4] As he adopts different voices and tries to amuse, entertain, and convince Éveline, he is simultaneously re-inventing his identity in a way which deals with his own past pain. As we shall see, letter-writing gives Balzac the opportunity not only to re-invent himself, but to return to an earlier state, returning to the 'there and then' — which is one of the possibilities offered by performance.[5]

In Chapter 1 we saw how Balzac does this in the sense that each new correspondence with a woman is essentially a 'return' to the original correspondence with his mother. Furthermore, in writing to Éveline, he claims that for him it is always 1833, that is, he wants them to write to each other as though they were still in the year when they met, thus betraying a desire to return to that earlier time.[6] This is just one example of how performance offers opportunities for what Schechner calls 'restored behaviour': 'Restored behaviour offers to both individuals and groups the chance to rebecome what they once were — or even, and most often, to rebecome what they never were but wish to have been or wish to become'.[7] This desire to use the letters to 'rebecome' something he had never in fact been, but wishes he could have been, is particularly evident in those letters in which Balzac writes for himself the part of Éveline's 'child'. In Chapter 1, we saw how Balzac claimed to Éveline that he never had a childhood before meeting her. From there, he progresses to casting himself as a child, and her as the mother. This allows him to play with the notion of 'first love' and portray himself in a non-threatening (non-sexual) light. Apparently relinquishing creative control in order to place himself in a passive, 'helpless' role, Balzac reverses the creative dynamic, ascribing to Éveline the role of matriarch and *auteur*. If Madame de Berny, described in earlier letters as Balzac's mother figure, was credited with having 'created' him (hers was, as Balzac phrased it, 'le cœur qui m'a créé' — the heart which created me), Balzac now tries to give Éveline to understand that she, in turn, has gained this creative power over him.[8]

Apparently relinquishing control also means that Balzac can refuse to accept blame for the imperfections of his relationships. Playing the child allows him to portray himself as a 'victim': 'un pauvre enfant, victime hier et encore victime demain de ses pudeurs de femme, de sa timidité' [a poor child, victim today and also tomorrow of his feminine prudishness, of his timidity].[9] Projecting this image of himself allows him to make strong statements: 'ne croyez à rien de mal de moi. Je suis un enfant, voilà tout, un enfant plus frivole que vous ne le croyez, mais pur comme un enfant, et aimant comme un enfant' [do not believe anything ill of me. I am a child, that is all, a child who is more frivolous than you think, yet pure as a child, and loving as a child].[10]

We see that this childlike persona can be put to good use in surprising ways. On 16 September 1834, Balzac wrote what must have been a somewhat difficult letter to Monsieur Hanski (Éveline's husband), apparently to explain why a love letter bearing his signature was found in Éveline's possession. The letter takes Balzac's 'caractère enfant et rieur' [childish, cheerful character] as his excuse, pretending that he had written her a fake love letter for fun.[11] The genius of this letter lies chiefly in the way Balzac pretends to be worried that he had offended Éveline with the 'joke' love letter, and boldly addresses himself to her husband as though he were an ally: 'Monsieur, je serais au désespoir si vous ne vouliez pas prendre ma défense auprès de Madame de Hanska [...] permettez-moi de vous expliquer, à vous la seule personne à qui je puisse en parler' [Monsieur, I would despair if you were not to defend me before Madame de Hanska [...] allow me to explain to you, the only person to whom I can speak of this].[12] Balzac then produces a charming sketch of his 'childishness', the character trait which, he claims, was at fault in the whole affair:

> Mais considérez un peu le caractère enfant et rieur que j'ai et sur lequel je ne me retrancherais pas si je ne vous l'avais fait connaître, et c'est parce que j'ai été près de vous comme je suis avec moi-même, avec la personne que j'aime le plus, que je me justifie.[13]

> [But just consider my childish, cheerful character, over which I would not be defending myself if I had not already made it known to you, and it is because I have behaved with you as I behave with myself, with the person I love the most, that I can justify myself.]

This address to the husband — very reminiscent of the ploy of the narrator of *Le Message* (1832), where careful flattery, and a feigned honesty, wins the narrator a private audience with another man's wife — is more than a downright lie: it is a carefully crafted performance of a previously perfected non-threatening role, which succeeds in pulling the wool over the complacent husband's eyes. Incredibly, the explanation must have seemed plausible enough, because there were no negative repercussions and Balzac was allowed to continue writing to Madame Hanska.

Balzac did appear to have a genuinely 'childlike' side, which was noted by his contemporaries. His sister Laure, too, referred to him later as an 'homme-enfant' [child at heart].[14] Éveline herself wrote in a letter to her brother that she found the great novelist to be very childlike, in terms of his unabashedness and sense of fun.[15] His contemporaries George Sand and Alphonse de Lamartine also commented on his 'childlike' qualities.[16] Critics have noted the extent to which Balzac enjoyed being 'childish'. Yet it is also true that Balzac carefully and deliberately cultivated a 'childlike' persona, especially in his correspondence with Madame Hanska:

> Je veux que vous vous disiez: — Il riait comme un enfant à Genève [...]! [...] Hé bien, c'est un enfant qui aime les cailloux, qui dit des bêtises, qui en fait, qui lit Gotha, qui fait des patiences et qui faisait rire M. de Hanski. Genève est pour moi un souvenir d'enfance.[17]

> [I want you to say to yourself: — He was laughing like a child in Geneva [...]! [...] Well, he is a child, who loves pebbles, who says stupid things, who does them, who reads Gotha, who plays patience and who made M. de Hanski laugh. Geneva is a childhood memory to me.]

Here, Balzac is not merely enjoying a happy memory of time spent with Madame Hanska. He is giving her a safe narrative with which to replace potentially negative narratives concerning their relationship. His comment 'Je veux que vous vous disiez' prescribes how she is to see him. It is important to bear in mind that this is a projection, a representation of Balzac as he would like to be viewed. In calling the time spent together in Geneva his 'childhood memory', Balzac is anchoring the relationship in this discourse of innocent love which runs through the whole correspondence.

Balzac plays on the various attributes of childhood, and performs this role in many of the ways that it is possible to be 'childlike'. At times he plays the pure and innocent child, as when he emphasizes his love.[18] At times he plays the vulnerable child, for instance when he calls himself her 'pauvre enfant' [poor child] after having felt himself mistreated.[19] On other occasions, playing the child helps him convey a childlike joy: 'ivre de bonheur, heureux, joyeux, dansant [...], sautant comme un enfant' [drunk with happiness, happy, joyful, dancing, [...] jumping about like a child].[20] When there is a possibility of spending six months in Madame Hanska's company, Balzac writes, 'Mon Dieu! Je crois que mon enfance revient!' [My God! I think my childhood has returned!].[21] In 1844, clearly intending to flatter, he confesses: 'Vous, chère Line, vous êtes *l'adorable enfance* que je n'ai pas eue' [You, dear Line, are *the adorable childhood* I never had].[22] His descriptions of himself as a 'child' cast an idyllic glow over his memories of time spent with her; for instance, his memory of their first meeting at Neuchâtel is described retrospectively as a sort of mother-child idyll:

> Oh que j'aurais voulu pouvoir rester une demi-journée à tes genoux, la tête dans tes genoux, rêvant de beaux rêves, te disant mes pensées avec paresse, avec délices, tantôt ne disant rien, mais baisant ta robe; mon Dieu que douce eut été cette journée où j'aurais pu jouer en liberté avec toi comme un enfant joue avec sa mère.[23]

> [Oh, how I would have liked to have been able to spend half the day at your knees, my head in your lap, dreaming beautiful dreams, lazily, delightedly telling you my thoughts; now and again saying nothing, but kissing your dress; my God, what sweetness there would have been in a day where I could have played with you freely, like a child plays with his mother.]

In a fantasy which essentially depicts two lovers, and which could be cast in a very sexual light, Balzac chooses to represent himself instead as a child at his mother's knee. Instead of depicting overt fantasies of adultery, he chooses the far less threatening images of a mother and child. Whereas in a letter to his sister Laure

Balzac had boasted of the 'baiser d'amour' [lovers' kiss] which was exchanged at Neuchâtel, in letters to Éveline he dwells instead on the pure, maternal connotations of their love.[24]

And this idea of the 'childish' first love spills into his novels. In *Eugénie Grandet*, for example, the novel which was to be triumphantly presented to Éveline in Geneva in 1833, the sleeping Charles momentarily 'rebecomes' a child when Eugénie touches him: 'il se laissa faire comme un enfant qui, même en dormant, connaît encore sa mère et reçoit, sans s'éveiller, ses soins et ses baisers' [he submitted to her caress like a child who, even whilst asleep, still knows his mother and receives her care and her kisses without waking up] (*CH*, III, 1122); and Eugénie takes on the role of the mother. Like Félix de Vandenesse, who blossoms during the second childhood that is his first love (in the section of *Le Lys dans la vallée* suitably entitled 'Les Deux Enfances' [The Two Childhoods]), Charles Grandet 'rebecomes' a child under the comforting influence of a first love. In *Eugénie Grandet*, Balzac explores certain similarities which he perceives between childhood and first love, both affected by the same pleasures, the same hopes, and the same quarrels:

> N'y a-t-il pas de gracieuses similitudes entre les commencements de l'amour et ceux de la vie? Ne berce-t-on pas l'enfant par de doux chants et de gentils regards? Ne lui dit-on pas de merveilleuses histoires qui lui dorent l'avenir? [...] Ne verse-t-il pas tour à tour des larmes de joie et de douleur? Ne se querelle-t-il pas pour des riens, pour des cailloux avec lesquels il essaie de se bâtir un mobile palais [...]? [...] L'amour est notre seconde transformation. (*CH*, III, 1135)

> [Are there not gracious similarities between the beginnings of love and the beginnings of life? Does one not soothe the child by soft singing and kind looks? Does one not tell him marvellous stories which gild the future for him? [...] Does he not spill tears of either joy or pain? Does he not argue over small things, over the pebbles with which he is trying to build himself a mobile palace [...]? [...] Love is our second transformation.]

These lines may well have been written with Madame Hanska's love in mind; as Robb points out, it was this novel which Balzac triumphantly offered to her in Vienna in 1833.[25] As we already know, Éveline Hanska was technically not Balzac's 'first love'. What is striking, however, is Balzac's insistence on this narrative where he and Éveline are 'first lovers' of sorts. In *Le Médecin de campagne,* a novel whose connection to Éveline Hanska has already been demonstrated, Balzac similarly muses: 'Le premier amour n'est-il pas une seconde enfance jetée à travers nos jours de peine et de labeur?' [Is not our first love just a second childhood, there to help us get through our daily grind?] (*CH*, IX, 546). This image of first love as a second childhood clearly haunts Balzac's literary imagination; reproduced across his novels and his correspondence with Éveline, it preoccupies and comforts Balzac until the end of his life: 'Je vous aime comme un fou', he writes to Éveline in September 1848, just before their final reunion, 'voici 8 jours que j'avance la tête pour vous voir comme les enfants qui tendent la main à leur mère avec ardeur, pendant qu'elle leur coupe du gâteau' [I love you like a madman [...], for 8 days now I keep lifting up my head to see you, as children stretch out their hand towards their mother fervently, while she cuts them a piece of cake].[26]

In the *Comédie humaine*, then, adult lovers are occasionally portrayed in a mother-child dynamic, and young men are seen to 'rebecome' children under the influence of a first love. What, then, of actual children in the *Comédie humaine* — who are very few and far between, and who do not appear to have much of a role to play?[27] We can think, for example, of little Wenceslas in *La Cousine Bette*, whom Wenceslas Steinbock 'creates' when he should be working on his statue; or the stillborn child of Valérie Marneffe, quietly buried without ceremony; or the child of Calyste and Sabine in *Béatrix*, who completes their happy family portrait at the end of the novel. These children are simply there, the fruit of a union between the more interesting adult protagonists, and themselves play no significant role. The one truly well-sketched portrait of a child in the *Comédie humaine* is Pierrette, the young protagonist of the novel of the same name, who eventually dies at the hands of her abusive relations.[28] Interestingly, this character can be seen as representative of the (adult) artist; more specifically, of Balzac himself. Véronique Bui points out that, like the artist, the heroine is a being still under formation,[29] and is therefore particularly vulnerable to the gaze of the Other, who, to paraphrase Bui, has the power either to petrify, decapitate, and suck out one's vital energy, or on the contrary, to allow the still-forming being to blossom.[30] Through Pierrette, Balzac apparently explored how the self can be affected by the way it is perceived, or interpreted, by the Other. In begging Éveline to recognize the 'child' in him, Balzac is insinuating that her ability to interpret him and his letters as she wishes is in fact a power to shape him. (It is of Pierrette that Balzac said 'Vous trouverez ici mille choses que j'ai à vous dire et que le papier ne me permet plus d'exprimer' [You will find in here a thousand things which I want to say, but which the paper no longer allows me to express].)[31]

Insofar as Madame Hanska was first and foremost a mother to her own little girl, Balzac's self-representation as her 'child' might be seen as a kind of rivalry. The way Balzac insinuates himself into her life is a little bit like the way Félix de Vandenesse works his way into the family life of Madame de Mortsauf, acting on occasion as though he were one of her children (for example, mimicking her children as he presents her with handpicked flowers, clamouring, just like the little ones do, for her approval).[32]

Most significantly, Balzac's portrayal of Éveline as 'maternal' links directly to Balzac's representation of her as a creator and maker. As Timothy Dobson points out, the role of the mother in the *Comédie humaine* is linked to creativity; a mother's children are her 'œuvres' [works].[33] As we see from Balzac's correspondence, he saw the romantic relationship as being similar to a mother-child relationship, in the sense that both have a strong 'creative' element to them (in his letters, we see the suggestion that lovers engage in what is essentially a process of mutual creation and re-creation).

The image of a child at the knees of his mother is only one in Balzac's catalogue of the purportedly 'inferior' roles he adopts. Balzac also enjoys the idea of himself as a serf, or 'mougick', at the control of his countess.[34] This playful image of himself is also yet another creative device, by means of which Balzac emphasizes Hanska's purported power over him, and yet emerges as the all-powerful creator himself; evidently, the dynamics of power in submission and dominance are not always what they appear to be.

The first letter in which Balzac imagines himself as Éveline's serf is written at the time of his stay in Geneva, during which a closer acquaintance with the Hanski family allowed Balzac to pick up on her ways, her quirks of pronunciation, and on her almost aristocratic way of life:

> Très chère souveraine, Majesté sacrée, sublime reine de Pawofka [*sic*] et lieux circonvoisins, autocrate des cœurs, rose d'Occident, Étoile du Nord, etc., etc.,
> etc., etc., etc.,
> fée des *tiyeuilles*!
> Votre grâce a désiré ma cafetière, et je supplie votre altesse sérénissime de me faire l'honneur d'en accepter une plus complète et plus jolie; puis de me dire, de jeter du haut de son trône éminentissime une parole pleine de bonheur, d'ambre, de fleurs, en me faisant savoir s'il faut se trouver à v[otre] sublime Porte avec la voiture pour aller à Coppet, dans une heure.
> Je dépose mes hommages aux pieds de votre Majesté et la supplie de croire à la probité de son
> humble mougik
> Honoreski.[35]

> [Very dear sovereign, sacred Majesty, sublime queen of Pawofka [*sic*] and surrounding areas, autocrat of hearts, rose of the East, star of the North, etc etc etc etc etc,
> Fairy of the *leenderns*!
> Your grace hath desireth my cafetiere, and I beg of your most serene highness to do me the honour of accepting one which is more complete and more attractive; and then to tell me, to cast down from your most eminent throne one simple word filled with happiness, with ambergris and flowers, by letting me know if I should find myself at y[our] sublime Door with the carriage, to go to Coppet in an hour.
> I leave my homage at your Majesty's feet and I beg of her to trust in the probity of her humble mougick
> Honoreski.]

In this very silly letter, Balzac mocks Madame Hanska's superior social status (possibly only just realizing the true extent of her superiority) and her speech — her mispronunciations of the word *tilleuls* [lindens] as 'tiyeuilles' (rendered here as 'leenderns') is one which Balzac liked so much that he inserted it into *Le Père Goriot*, 'en riant comme un fou' [laughing like a madman], and also mimicked repeatedly in the correspondence.[36] Yet what could have been pure mockery here takes the form of exaggerated worship of a princess. This idea of his servitude provides an interesting counterpart to the dynamic of control which this study has so far identified in his letters, and to the idea of him as a controlling maker. It is also from this time onwards that Balzac openly begins to imitate Éveline's speech; he takes a clear delight in her Slavic pronunciation and will henceforth reproduce it in the letters phonetically. Balzac thus not only adopts a new role, but a new voice, trying to get closer to the linguistic and cultural landscape into which she was born. The sounds of her language, so far new to him, now begin to influence him. 'J'ai rêvé ka, j'ai rêvé ki, j'ai rêvé tchef' [I dreamt of *ka*, I dreamt of *ki*, I dreamt of *tschef*], he writes in 1835 of the sounds that have got under his skin.[37] Imitating her voice produces the illusion of her proximity. 'Quand j'ai un instant à moi, que je suis trop fatigué pour écrire, [...] je me reporte à Genève, je prononce machinalement *tyeuille*, et je m'illusionne' [When I have a moment to myself, and I am too tired to write, [...] I think back to Geneva, I pronounce *leenderns* automatically, and I lose myself in dreams].[38]

This idea of himself as the faithful serf and her as 'the sovereign' is one he takes a liking to. He takes pleasure in referring to himself in the third person, for instance when asking for permission to go into society: 'Le mougick ira là tous les 15 jours, si la dame le lui permet' [The mougick will go there once a fortnight, if the lady permits him].[39] There is a clear element of storytelling here, with Balzac inventing the story of a faithful servant and his lady. In another passage he appears like a downtrodden hero in a fairy tale, who in reality has superpowers: 'je vous tiens au courant des grandes opérations de votre dévoué mougick' [I shall keep you apprised of the great operations of your devoted mougick]; the phrase 'grandes opérations' implies great and secretive doings, perhaps on her behalf, and of whose scale she is not even aware.[40] When he reprimands her over what he sees as unfounded suspicions about his fidelity, he falls at her feet in the guise of her faithful serf once more; in this instance, 'mougick' fittingly replaces a more traditional, old-fashioned salutation such as 'devoted servant':

> Oh ceci n'est pas bien, surtout quand il s'agit de quelqu'un qui vous est dévoué de tout point, comme l'est votre pauvre
> mougick
> Honoré de Bc.[41]

> [Oh this will not do, especially as we are speaking of someone who is devoted to you in everything, as is your
> nougick
> Honoré de Bc.]

Early biographers have taken issue with this dynamic, suggesting Balzac was unnecessarily prostrating himself before Éveline's superior social status.[42] Yet clearly there is far more at stake here. This apparent fantasy of subservience is in fact a fantasy of his own hidden intellectual superiority. The *mougick* can be seen as a reinterpretation of the 'fool' (in French, *bouffon*, or *fou*), another literary figure of servitude and devotion, often underappreciated and misunderstood — a character whom Balzac played early on in the correspondence, before he had the Slavic vocabulary to draw on. Both these frequently used tropes, the *mougick* and the fool, are motifs of subservience; and yet, in Balzac's representation of them, both have superior insights and hidden strengths of character. It is the *mougick*-fool who has the potential to rescue the princess, if only she would let him.

> Faites acheter à M. de H[anski] une principauté, car je ne voudrais pas être bouffon si je n'étais pas à un prince. Il faut concilier les amours-propres. Vous me donneriez des bonnets très jolis, quant à mes appointements, je les trouverais dans les rires que je verrais sur vos lèvres. Mais vous serez tenue de me donner des éloges et une loge, des sonnettes et un gâteau. Point de barkschz, je fais mes conditions. Puis le fou vous cachera son cœur. Allons vous ne voudriez pas de moi. Puis j'aurais peur que ma folie ne soit pas en moi.[43]

> [Tell M. de Hanski to buy a principality, for I would not want to be a fool unless I belonged to a prince. We must satisfy my vanities. You will give me

some very pretty hats, and as for my salary, this I shall draw from the laughter that comes from your lips. But you will need to give me plenty of praise, a dressing room, bells, and a cake. No barktsch please, I must put my foot down. But then the fool will hide his heart from you. At that point, you will no longer want me. And then I would be afraid that my madness truly is within me.]

This passage is an example of a particularly well-crafted *mise en abyme*. Through the story of himself as the fool, Balzac becomes at once the character in the story and the storyteller; he is both the amusing poet and the serious, earnest correspondent. In taking on all these roles, he leaves no space uncovered. Moreover, the image of the fool, with its link to madness, and its connotations of the eccentric — a word which in itself suggests one who is decentralized, exterior to, be it the centre of society, or the realm of rational language — is suggestive of the language of madness, dangerous, potentially worrying, yet interesting and often amusing. In literature (we need only think of the example of *King Lear*) the fool is often discredited, and is usually the character whom no-one takes seriously, who always tells the truth, and who, because he always speaks in jest, goes largely unpunished.

In describing himself as the court jester of the Hanskis, thus decentralizing himself and placing himself outside the realm of society and conventional language, Balzac adds yet more force to the rhetoric of control already present in the letters. He implies that he is aware of more undercurrents of meaning in their relationship than she is. Inspiring pity and yet at the same time amusing and wise, Balzac's *bouffon* prefigures the 'nain mystérieux' [mysterious dwarf] of *Modeste Mignon*, Jean Butscha, the ardent admirer of the young heroine, who, despite his superior talents and insights, remains forever on the outside of all correspondence, confidences, and love affairs.

Balzac can also be seen performing for Madame Hanska at a more obvious level. In later years of the correspondence, when she travels through Europe together with the now-married Anna and the latter's husband, Georges Mniszech, Balzac's letters begin to speak of the four of them as a troupe of 'saltimbanques' [entertainers], with himself as their leader (he re-christens all the members of the family with new 'stage names'; his own is 'Bilboquet'). Balzac's self-representation as a performer chimes with the troubling idea of an artist being reduced to a public performance; yet in his appropriation and reworking of these loaded artistic terms — 'bouffon', 'saltimbanque' — he manages somehow to subvert the established social hierarchies. Normally, for an artist to represent himself as a 'saltimbanque' would be to embrace the destiny of the outcast.[44] In this instance, however, Balzac is more ambiguous, as he is drawing Éveline and her family into his imaginary world. They are all outcasts, performers, travelling artists, together. The discourse of Balzac as a performer, which runs throughout the entire correspondence, possesses a cultural resonance which had currency at the time, and which Balzac appropriated and reworked; voluntarily casting himself out of society and yet in this instance creating ambiguity as he attempts to entice the others to follow him into his symbolic exile, he is all at once the *bouffon*-truth-teller and the creator-fabulist.[45]

II

As I have already suggested, Balzac plays these roles intermittently, adopting them and changing them at will in his seduction of Madame Hanska. The more playful roles, such as the child and the *mougick* discussed above, offset his role as Éveline's admirer, helping his cause in that they stop his portrayal of himself as her suitor from becoming overbearing. The 'époux d'amour' [husband in love] is a role which sits well with Balzac's function as a director; these roles, both of which are linked to control, spill over into one another. Already at the first meeting in Neuchâtel, a promise of marriage (of sorts) was made: as Balzac wrote to Laure, 'J'ai juré d'attendre, et *elle* de me réserver sa main, son cœur' [I promised to wait, and *she* to reserve me her hand, her heart].[46] As early as 1833, Balzac begins calling Madame Hanska his 'épouse d'amour' [bride in love], laying claim to her as his future wife.[47]

In his letters, Balzac appears to be putting down in writing what was verbally promised at Neuchâtel — implying that, in his mind, the binding part of the marriage contract had already taken place. 'Oui, je vis en toi comme tu vis en moi. Jamais Dieu ne séparera ce qu'il a si fort assemblé. Ma vie est ta vie' [Yes, I live in you, as you live in me. Those whom God has joined together he would never put asunder. My life is your life], he wrote in December 1833, and we note the striking similarity of this phrase to that of the traditional wording of a marriage ceremony.[48] As we have already seen, Madame Hanska had confessed to Balzac very early on that her marriage was loveless. Balzac apparently took this as his cue to reassure her of the irrelevance, legally, morally, or otherwise, of the presence of the husband to their personal plans: his letters suggest that, in his opinion, the 'contract' between himself and Hanska is more sacred and binding than a marriage contract. Her worries over her perceived infidelity in writing to Balzac are quickly brushed aside. 'Vous me parlez d'une infidèle, mais il n'y a pas d'infidélité quand il n'y a pas eu amour' [You talk to me of an unfaithful woman, but there is no infidelity where there was no love], he writes early on in the correspondence, refuting her anxieties in one fell swoop, with not even a direct mention of her husband.[49] Indeed, Balzac the dramatist begins literally to write Monsieur Hanski out of the 'script' altogether. There is no room in the Balzac-Hanska love story for an unfaithful woman lumbered with an ageing husband.

Instead, Balzac begins to write for Éveline the part of the virginal bride. When for example he describes kissing her, this kiss is represented as her first: 'Un baiser sur tes lèvres chéries, ces lèvres vierges qui n'ont point de souvenirs encore (et ce qui te rend à mes yeux pure comme la jeune fille la plus pure)' [One kiss on your dear lips, those virgin lips which as yet have no memories (and this makes you, in my eyes, as pure as the purest young girl)].[50] Balzac is thus not only writing Éveline's entire sexual past out of existence; in staging her as a virginal beauty, he invites her to 'rebecome' what she once was, or wished she could have been.[51] He will perform the part of her first lover.

In attempting to cement his position as rightful husband, one of the things Balzac does is try to create a bond between himself and Éveline's daughter, Anna. Balzac sends small presents for the child, including a cross which he had specially made for her, using stones she herself had gathered on a walk. Balzac expressly states his desire that Anna should wear this cross, and that he intends for Éveline to see it every day around the neck of her child and think of him:

> Ma chère épouse d'amour, qu'Anna porte la petite croix que je vais faire faire avec ses cailloux; je ferai graver derrière *adoremus in aeternum*, c'est une délicieuse devise de femme, et tu ne pourras pas voir cette croix sans penser à celui qui te dira sans cesse ces divines paroles par ce petit talisman de jeune fille.[52]

> [My dear wife-in-love, make Anna wear the little cross which I am having made out of her pebbles; I will have *adoremus in aeternum* engraved on it, a beautiful feminine motto, and you will not be able to see this cross without thinking of the one who will never cease to tell you these divine words by means of that girlish talisman.]

The 'girlish talisman' is clearly intended to mean more to Éveline Hanska than it is to Anna. Balzac implied that the proposed motto of 'adoremus in aeternum' was his and Éveline's alone,[53] but it was very likely recycled from a previous love affair.[54] Ostensibly an appropriate thing to engrave on a cross, it is in fact highly subversive, referring less to the adoration of Christ than to illicit love affairs. There is perhaps something distasteful in insisting on hanging this symbol, which links Balzac and her mother, around the neck of the child. In suggesting that Éveline will not be able to view this cross without being reminded of him, Balzac is subtly undermining the paternity of Monsieur Hanski. Whilst the child is a physical reminder of the union of Madame Hanska and her legal husband, Balzac effectively tries to change this by making himself visible and present in the daily life of Madame Hanska, turning her daughter into a living reminder of him.

Balzac makes the pebble cross into a symbolic object, invested with an almost sacred weight. 'J'ai renvoyé les restes de cailloux, je n'avais pas le droit de perdre ce qu'a touché, ramassé Anna' [I sent back the rest of the pebbles, I did not have the right to squander something that Anna had touched and gathered], writes Balzac, speaking of Anna's pebbles as sacrosanct, a relic.[55] He humorously emphasizes what effort it cost him to find a jeweller who might be able to set the stones:

> Avant que le sublime Fossin ait daigné quitter les diadèmes, les couronnes des princes, pour sertir les cailloux ramassés par votre fille, il a fallu bien prier, bien s'humilier, quitter souvent ma retraite où je suis occupé à sertir de pauvres phrases.[56]

> [Before the sublime Fossin would deign to leave behind his diadems and his princely crowns, in order to set the pebbles gathered by your daughter, I had to beg, lower myself, leave my retreat very often, where I am busy setting my humble phrases.]

Anna's pebbles, treated in the same way as fine jewels — and Balzac's precious words — acquire a special significance in Balzac's literary imagination, gaining a similar, performative, function to that of his 'phrases'. The pebbles become a recurrent motif which harks back to an earlier experience, much as a recurring prop in a play serves to guide the audience subconsciously towards a feeling previously evoked.[57]

We have already seen how Balzac makes reference to himself as an agreeable boy who likes playing with stones.[58] There are further references to pebbles both in Balzac's correspondence and in his novels, each one evoking the innocence and simplicity of childhood. In the *Comédie humaine,* references to pebbles evoke the nostalgia of an earlier time. In *La Peau de chagrin,* Raphaël de Valentin laments the fact that his life has been a lie: like his creator, Balzac, he too spent his life 'constamment assis, une plume à la main' [always seated, pen in hand], whereas he would have liked to 'faire, comme un enfant, ricocher des cailloux sur l'eau' [skim stones on the water, like a child] (*CH*, x, 139). Félix de Vandenesse spends some of the happier moments of his lonely childhood 'à jouer avec des cailloux' [playing with pebbles] (*CH*, IX, 971). In *La Dernière Fée ou la nouvelle lampe merveilleuse,* which portrays a most idyllic childhood, we are told that 'six cailloux et de la boue' [six pebbles and some mud] are the only toys a child needs (*PR*, II, 29).

The recurrence of this cherished symbol in Balzac's novels, often predating the Hanska correspondence, renders his insistence on this symbol in the letters all the more meaningful. The stones symbolize not only childhood pleasures, but also have obvious connotations with building, creating, and imagining, in the way a child creates a whole world of its own. When he describes to Éveline his preliminary searches for beautiful objects with which to fill their future home, Balzac describes this house, too, as 'cette maison de cailloux que tous les enfants ont construite' [that house made of stones which all children have constructed].[59] Through this recurrent image, Balzac brings together the themes of creativity and childhood in surprising ways.

Seen within Balzac's dynamic of performance, the cross with its pebbles becomes an objective correlative, evoking a symbol of the early days of the relationship with Éveline. The 'cailloux de l'allée du milieu du jardin de la maison Mirabaud où n[ous] n[ous] promenions' [stones from the alley in the middle of the Mirabaud garden where we once walked], the imaginary 'stones' out of which Balzac builds his dream house, all recall those 'cailloux de la route de Ferney' [pebbles on the road to Ferney] which Anna gathered, and in exchange for which Balzac claims he would willingly give up 'la gloire et tout mon baggage littéraire' [glory and all my literary baggage].[60] This recurrent prop ties together childhood, love, and creativity, and, in making a passing allusion to these themes, creates the possibility of a fleeting return to a time, as such symbols do in theatrical performance.

Through the use of this, and other such 'props', Balzac begins setting the stage for his fantasy of himself and Madame Hanska as husband and wife. His later letters to Éveline and to his mother show a preoccupation — we might even say an obsession — with objects purchased to furnish his new house in the rue Fortunée, in which he and Madame Hanska were to live as man and wife.[61] We know that Balzac was fond of dressing up and using specific props — such as his famous turquoise cane — to help him play a particular role in society.[62] Certain gifts he sends, or intends to send, to Éveline, seem to help Balzac stay in character. Setting the stage for their future marriage, already in 1834 Balzac writes that he wants to fill her home with objects similar to the ones he sees and handles on a daily basis:

J'ai fait faire un si admirable flambeau à 3 branches que je voudrais t'envoyer le pareil, de même que je te voudrais un encrier, un réveil (chose bien utile à une femme) enfin tout ce dont je me sers, semblable chez toi. [...] Oh je suis gourmet, affamé de ces choses qui mettent sans cesse deux amants au cœur l'un de l'autre. A W[ierzchownia], je ferai faire ta chambre semblable à la mienne, je te veux le même tapis.[63]

[I have had such an adorable lamp made, with three branches, that I would like to send you one just the same, just as I would like to send you an inkwell, an alarm clock (a useful thing for a woman), well, everything I use — I would like you to have the same in your home. [...] Oh, I am greedy, starved of those things which place two lovers ceaselessly in one another's heart. At W[ierzchownia] I will have your room decorated like mine, I want you to have the same carpet.]

Through his letters, Balzac can imagine turning Éveline's living space into a stage set of his own home, writing the theatrical decor of the space he would like her to inhabit — *his* space. It is also interesting that he should desire her to inhabit a space artificially constructed by him, in view of the fact that, in an early letter, he had begged her for a 'copie fidèle de la chambre où vous écrivez, où vous pensez, où vous êtes *vous,* car vous le savez, il y a des moments où nous sommes plus nous, où il n'y a plus de masque' [faithful replica of the bedroom where you write, where you think, where you are *yourself,* for as you know, there are some moments when we are more ourselves, where we no longer wear a mask].[64] The decor of the room where Éveline is 'herself', where she takes off the 'mask' which society requires her to wear, would ideally be directed by him.

While it is, of course, impossible for Balzac to realize this fantasy of shipping identical furnishings all the way to the Ukraine, what he can do is delight in planning and visualizing such a space in his letters, and to use them to hint to her that his home has been imbued with her presence. 'C'est toi partout, matériellement parlant' [You are everywhere, materially speaking], he writes in 1845, as he describes the array of mementoes of her which he has collected over the years, and which are arranged before him as he writes.[65] On another occasion, remembering how she wore a violet dress at Neuchâtel, Balzac describes how he filled his home with flashes of violet, thus 'staging' her presence through the physical presence of the colour: 'Depuis ce jour, mon petit salon a été violet, j'ai aimé le violet, et il m'en reste une perse violette, une table couverte d'un drap violet et des torsades violettes qui sont des reliques pour moi!' [Ever since that day, my little sitting-room has been violet, I have loved the colour violet, and I still have some violet draperies, a table covered with a violet cloth, and some violet curtain trimmings which are like relics for me!].[66] He is thus suggesting that, just as he would like to fill her interior with flashes of his existence, she has likewise had an influence on his; he hints that she has a hand in the running of his household, though in fact she remains conspicuously absent.

The colour violet, used here to evoke Madame Hanska's presence in his life, recalls not only the violet dress but other flashes of violet — such as the dried violets exchanged in the early correspondence. In 1833, he sent her a violet from his garden, claiming that it symbolized his love.[67] When Madame Hanska reciprocated with a violet of her own, Balzac criticized the fact that hers was not scented, adding, 'Je t'envoie une violette de mon jardin' [I am sending you a violet from my garden].[68] It is not, it would seem, that Hanska's violet was inferior to his; rather, he wished to be in charge of how the flower is used in his *mise en scène* of their relationship. Then there are those violets written into Balzac's fiction, which come to symbolize a fragile and unattainable love. I am thinking particularly of *Séraphîta* and *Honorine*, two novels in which the violet is a symbol of beauty and fragility, and also unattainability. In *Séraphîta*, the youthful Minna is compared to 'la violette cachée au pied du chêne' [the violet hidden at the foot of an oak tree]; she would die if the bright sun were to 'éclairer' [shine on] her (*CH*, XI, 745). The eponymous heroine of *Honorine* (likewise a fragile young woman) exhales a 'parfum de violette' [scent of violets], and is described as a 'violette ensevelie dans sa forêt de fleurs' [violet hidden away in her forest of flowers], happy in her shaded hiding place (*CH*, II, 564 & 567). When she is dragged from her safe haven and out into the harsh 'light', she perishes. Honorine, who excites the senses like a 'violet' — 'une fleur pour le toucher, une fleur pour le regard, une fleur pour l'odorat, une fleur céleste pour l'âme' [a flower to the touch, a flower to the gaze, a flower to the nose, a celestial flower to the soul] (*CH*, II, 564) — recalls Éveline in the violet dress which so tantalized Balzac. Perhaps Balzac was romanticizing her unattainability, imagining her as the hidden violet which should not be enticed out into the light. As Jeannine Guichardet notes, Balzac's use of traditional flower clichés in his letters to Madame Hanska ('fleur céleste' [celestial flower], 'fleur de ma vie' [flower of my life]) takes on a new lease of life during the period in which Balzac wrote *Honorine*.[69]

Balzac's affinity for playing the role of masked seducer (explored in Chapter 1) is another parallel between his life and the story of Honorine. In *Honorine*, the heroine is enticed into adultery, and runs away from her husband to live briefly with a man who later abandons her. We know almost nothing about Honorine's seducer, who, although invisible, is of course an important catalyst for much of the playacting which ensues.[70] In his letters, Balzac appears to enjoy playing such a hidden persona. Ostensibly remaining respectful and courting Monsieur Hanski under the guise of esteemed family friend, sending gifts of manuscripts and autographs, Balzac also makes some overtures which verge on the inappropriate. When he sends Éveline the gift of a letter-knife, he writes, 'Je me suis occupé de votre couteau à papier et de votre porte-plume, j'ai pensé que [...] M. de H[anski] permettrait à l'amitié d'empiéter sur ses droits' [I have seen to your paper-knife and your penholder, I thought that [...] M. de Hanski would not mind a friend encroaching upon his rights].[71] (We can glean from this that perhaps Monsieur Hanski was supposed to buy her this present, but Balzac went ahead and bought it first.)

This ostensibly innocuous comment conceals a whole dimension of masks and assumed identities. This letter is a double stab in the back for Hanski, whose wife is having a love affair with its sender. Thus in fact Balzac plays a dual role, for at the same time as playing the double-crossing seducer he also performs the function of the stage director. Balzac orchestrates a situation where Monsieur Hanski is placed unwittingly in the position of the ignorant cuckold, and Éveline momentarily becomes the spectator, the audience member who is in on the seducer's secret and, unlike the unsuspecting husband on stage, can appreciate the full irony of the scene (and the somewhat phallic nature of the gift). The letter marks the theatrical boundary between those who are in on the essential secret, and those who suspect nothing.

Exchanges of gifts become part and parcel of Balzac's epistolary 'play'. We see Balzac demanding from Éveline specific gifts, which have a symbolic or representative function. In the same letter in which he expresses his disappointment with her unscented violet, he suggests that a piece of white ribbon would be of more use to him next time.[72] We note from this request that not only is he trying to control what he receives, but he also seems to want objects which have, or could have been, worn on the body. The piece of grey silk from a dress which Éveline had worn in Geneva, and which he requests for the binding of *Séraphîta*, thus creating a symbolic union of their two bodies, is one such example: 'Il [le manuscrit de *Séraphîta*] sera grossièrement relié, avec le drap gris qui glissait si bien sur les planchers. Ne suis je pas un peu femme, hein, minette?' [It [the manuscript of *Séraphîta*] will be roughly bound, with that grey cloth which slid so well over the floorboards. Am I not a little bit like a woman, eh, darling?].[73]

In 1843, he also begs for another piece of silk (black this time) from Éveline's dress, so that he can use it to wipe his pen:

> Ah! j'ai une prière à vous faire; c'est de m'envoyer, par une de vos lettres, un fragment d'une robe de soie, quelque chose comme du foulard, de couleur foncée, un lambeau que vous jetteriez, et avec quoi j'essuyerai ma plume. Cette petite chose que je manie à chaque instant, me ferait plaisir si elle venait de vous.[74]

> [Ah! I have a favour to beg of you; it is to send me, in one of your letters, a fragment from a silk dress, something like a scarf, dark-coloured, a scrap that you might otherwise throw away, and with which I shall wipe my pen. This little thing which I shall handle all the time would bring me pleasure if it were to come from you.]

The piece of dark silk as part of the paraphernalia of writing, the manuscript 'dressed up' in a fragment of Éveline's clothing, the sexual implication of the pen wiped on the dress: these examples show that Balzac is setting up the writing process itself as a kind of performance, a daily ritual which is to be staged as one of the rites and ceremonies of carnal love. In writing his letters to Éveline, Balzac portrays himself as thinking constantly of the mistress, managing to prevent these somewhat sexualized requests from seeming inappropriate; he seems to achieve this through alternating between the roles he plays. When he offers Éveline the letter-knife, he plays the devoted family friend. When he asks for a piece of her grey dress for his manuscript — even with the clearly erotic image of Éveline's body which the cloth represents, and the secret which it colludes in and which it cloaks ('le drap gris qui glissait si bien sur les planchers') — Balzac tempers the potentially inappropriate fantasy by immediately adopting a non-threatening role: 'Ne suis je pas un peu femme, hein, minette?'].

We remember that Madame Hanska did not like his portrayal of 'femmes fatales' in *La Peau de chagrin*, urging him to return instead to the virtuous roles he wrote for women in his *Scènes de la vie de province*.[75] Balzac shows an ability to maintain his respect for her conception of feminine virtue by never overtly writing to her in a way which might seem salacious and disrespectful. He is careful not to treat her as a femme fatale, yet his writing nonetheless expresses, in myriad ways, his sexual desire for her, all the while making it sound as though she were the dominant force in the relationship, as though these ideas were coming from her in the first place.

III

With this in mind, we can see that it may be partly in response to a comment by Madame Hanska, which suggests that she appreciates his understanding of women, that Balzac insists so much on his 'feminine' side in this correspondence. In her letter dated 7 November 1832, Madame Hanska had described her reaction to the sensitive portrayal of women in some of his novels:

> En lisant vos ouvrages mon cœur a tressailli; vous élevez la femme à sa juste dignité; l'amour chez elle est une vertu céleste, une émanation divine; j'admire en vous cette admirable sensibilité d'âme qui vous l'a fait deviner. [...] Du moment où je lus vos ouvrages, je m'identifiai à vous, à votre génie.[76]

> [While I was reading your works, my heart trembled with joy; you raise up the woman to her rightful level of dignity; love is a celestial virtue to her, a divine emanation; I admire in you this admirable sensitivity of your soul which made you guess this correctly. [...] From the moment I read your works I identified with you, with your genius.]

Balzac appears to echo some of these sentiments by replying: 'Tout ce que la femme rêve de plus délicat et de plus romanesque trouve en mon cœur, non pas un écho, mais une simultanéité incroyable de pensée' [Everything that the woman might dream of that is delicate and romantic will find not only an echo in my own heart, but also an incredible simultaneity of thought].[77] Balzac seems to take Éveline's praise as his cue to demonstrate his feminine sensibility. His attempt to portray himself as feminine may be regarded as an attempt to get closer to her by claiming a similarity of feeling and experience. From the few of her letters that remain, we can see that Balzac's assertions on this point try to mirror hers. She claims never to have been in love; he responds with lengthy descriptions of his bare and monastic existence, of how he has lived 'sans avoir été aimé par une jeune et jolie femme' [without ever having been loved by a young and beautiful woman].[78] She calls herself 'simple et vraie, mais timide et craintive' [simple and true, yet timid and fearful];[79] he obliges with a similarly charming picture of himself as a 'victime hier et encore victime demain de ses pudeurs de femme, de sa timidité, de ses croyances' [a victim, today and still tomorrow, of his feminine modesty, of his timidity, of his beliefs].[80] She speaks of 'le sentiment qui m'anime, l'Amour!' [the feeling which makes me come alive, Love!],[81] and he in turn affirms that 'Aimer, Éva, c'est ma vie' [To love, Eva, is my life].[82] We see from these echoes of her words that Balzac's claims to femininity are to an extent modelled on what she has already told him about herself. Claiming that a high level of mutual comprehension exists between them, he says 'vous vous adressez à un esprit tout féminin' [you are addressing a completely feminine mind].[83] His artistic sensitivity towards women having drawn her to him, Balzac draws the two personae of the artist and the woman together in the way he presents himself to her, saying: 'Il n'y a que les artistes qui soient dignes des femmes, parce qu'ils sont un peu femmes' [There is no one but artists who are worthy of women, because they themselves are a little bit female].[84]

In assuaging Éveline's worries about the other women in his life, Balzac compares his feelings on this subject to those of a woman.[85] When asking for kindness and understanding, Balzac again pleads feminine sensitivity: 'ne me maltraite pas, j'ai le cœur tout aussi sensible que peut l'être celui d'une femme' [do not treat me harshly, my heart is just as sensitive as a woman's heart can be].[86] Furthermore, Balzac claims that his love has a special quality precisely because of his ability to play different roles simultaneously: 'crois-moi, je t'aime à la fois comme aime une femme et comme aime un homme' [believe me, I love you at the same time as a woman loves and as a man loves].[87]

It is this crucial idea which finds its way into Balzac's *Séraphîta*. It is no coincidence that Balzac conceived of this work at a time when he was trying to convince Éveline that he was capable of loving her with both the love of a woman and the love of a man. Balzac insinuated that this novel was more than just a work which touches the two of them; indeed, it *was* them. '*Séraphîta*, c'est nous deux', he wrote to Éveline, 'déployons donc nos ailes par un seul et même mouvement, aimons de la même manière' [*Séraphîta* is the two of us, so let us spread our wings using one and the same movement, let us love in the same way].[88] *Séraphîta* is thus described as a direct projection of the Balzac–Hanska relationship.

In the dedication of *Séraphîta*, Balzac hinted that the novel was written at Éveline's request, implying that she played a significant role in the creative process.[89] Yet we know that the idea for *Séraphîta* came to Balzac independently, during a visit to the studio of a sculptor, albeit under the influence of his new relationship with Éveline.[90] In his notebook *Pensées, sujets, fragments* Balzac wrote 'Prendre pour épigraphe *adoremus in aeternum*' [Use as epigraph *adoremus in aeternum*].[91] This motto, which, as we have seen, had already been used as a device in the correspondence with Éveline, and prior to that in a novel, shows to what extent this novel was in fact bound up with his earlier ideas and correspondence.

Scholars have of course remarked on the link between this work and Balzac's relationship with Madame Hanska, but for the most part have not explored this in great depth. For instance, in her latest study of this novel, by way of summarizing the relevance of the story to the relationship between Balzac and Madame Hanska, Anne-Marie Baron simply comments that it proposed a 'vision idéale du couple humain qui comble l'amoureux de Mme Hanska' [an ideal vision of the human couple which greatly pleased Mme Hanska's lover].[92]

Yet the relation of this novel to Balzac's correspondence with Éveline needs to be analyzed more carefully. *Séraphîta* was not simply a part of Balzac's attempt to show Éveline to what extent he was capable of understanding the female psyche; nor was it simply 'une consécration de leur amour' [a consecration of their love] (*CH*, XI, 1624, n. 1). The novel is essentially about one character's ability to perform different roles and selves, and as such it is a reflection of the role-playing dynamic in the letters to Éveline. It is no coincidence that Balzac insisted on including her maiden name ('Née comtesse Rzewuska') alongside her married name in the dedication. In this novel which alludes to the possibility of 'rebecoming' what one once was, or wished to have been, this early allusion to Madame Hanska's former identity already introduces this as the novel's key theme. This novel, ostensibly Balzac's attempt to showcase his 'two natures', in fact reveals Balzac-Séraphîta as a would-be supreme dramatist, actor, theatre director, and even prompter (in French, *souffleur*); it is through her breath (*souffle*), that Séraphîta communicates to Minna and Wilfrid the attitudes she would like them to take.[93]

The novel opens like a play — with light after a period of darkness. In setting the scene in Norway, Balzac exploits the analogy of the dark theatre bursting into light, and of the spectators finally being allowed to watch the show. The 'vaste miroir des eaux réfléchissant les couleurs du ciel' [vast mirror of waters, reflecting the colours of the sky] is described as a 'spectacle curieux' [curious spectacle], which 'Depuis longtemps il n'avait pas été permis aux gens de Jarvis de voir' [For a long time the people of Jarvis were not permitted to see] (*CH*, XI, 734). On the morning when Séraphîtus (Séraphîta's male alter ego) and Minna climb the Falberg, this 'stage' is brightly lit: 'le soleil éclatait au sein de ce paysage en y allumant les feux de tous les diamants éphémères [...] de la neige et des glaces' [the sun was breaking out in the heart of this landscape, illuminating all with the dazzle of the ephemeral diamonds [...] of ice and snow] (*CH*, XI, 735). Very likely it is not for its glacial monstrosity that Balzac chose Norway as the setting, which is the claim put forward by Juliette Frølich, but rather for the analogy with the lifting of a (theatre) curtain, of the long darkness followed by light, which this landscape offers.[94] This analysis becomes all the more plausible if we consider how much emphasis there is on light. The play of light, which bursts forth 'par moments' [here and there], almost blinding the spectator, recalls the play of lights in a theatre (*CH*, XI, 735); and there is a curtain of sorts, which rises and falls, represented through 'des amas de nuées grises [...] [qui] cachaient le ciel sous de triples voiles' [clusters of grey cloud [...] hiding the sky behind a threefold veil] (*CH*, XI, 734–35). In the midst of all this, the actor-director Séraphîta points out the theatrical framework of the scene, and consequently of the whole novel:

> Mais ne sois pas injuste, Minna, vois le spectacle qui s'étale à tes pieds, n'est-il pas grand? A tes pieds, l'Océan se déroule comme un tapis, les montagnes sont comme les murs d'un cirque, l'éther est au-dessus comme le voile arrondi de ce théâtre, et d'ici l'on respire les pensées de Dieu comme un parfum. Vois? (*CH*, XI, 744)

> [But do not be unfair, Minna, see the spectacle which is unfolding at your feet, is it not grand? At your feet, the ocean is unfolding like a carpet, the mountains are like the walls of a circus, the ether is above them like the rounded curtain of this theatre, and from here we can breathe in God's very thoughts like a fragrance. You see?]

Unravelling before her like a carpet, the world at Minna's feet seems to be inviting her to enter into the theatre and participate in it, should she choose to. Joan Dargan, in discussing this passage, correctly observes that here Séraphîtüs 'sees the world as his creator sees it: the theatre for the *Comédie humaine*'; however she then claims that he and Minna are both at this moment 'too far removed' from the world they are viewing, and so the individual dramas of the world below are lost on Séraphîtüs. Dargan simply notes that afterwards Séraphîtüs leads Minna down from the mountain, and that his 'exaltation is utterly prosaic'.[95] Yet rather than view the characters' descent from the mountain as an act of turning away, we can view it as a preparation for taking on new roles, for immersing themselves in this world which is their stage.

That their roles have changed is signalled, somewhat crudely, when we are told that 'Séraphîtüs commença à laisser sa force mâle et à dépouiller ses regards de leur trop vive intelligence' [Séraphîtüs began to leave behind his male force and his glances began to lose their too-keen intelligence] (*CH*, XI, 747), and when Minna, who up until now seems to have been in the company of a young man, addresses her friend using 'chère' (the feminine form of 'my dear') (Ibid.). Up on the Falberg, Séraphîtüs-Séraphîta alternates between the roles of tormentor and friend, and these changes are signified by a change of voice. Like an actor (and like Balzac, who tried a variety of 'voices' in his relationship with Madame Hanska), Séraphîta changes her voice at will, from that of an eagle to a turtledove (*CH*, XI, 746), to a 'voix pure comme celle d'une jeune fille et qui dissipa les lueurs fantastiques du songe' [voice as pure as a young girl's, and which dispersed the fairytale glow of the dream] (*CH*, XI, 747). As in a theatre, changes of light in *Séraphîta* tend to signal a radical redefinition of scenes and incarnations; for instance, the transformation of Séraphîtus into Séraphîta begins as the daylight starts to fade (*CH*, XI, 746–47).

Séraphîta's changing gender has particularly baffled past readers. 'En a-t-il fait un être asexué ou bisexué?' [Did he make her into an asexual or bisexual being?], ponders one critic.[96] Balzac deliberately upholds the ambiguity. Yet what is more interesting is the way he uses this character to highlight the accepted performances, in society, of the two separate gender roles. When Wilfrid contemplates the theatrical tableau with Séraphîta, 'la séduisante créature qui gisait étendue à ses yeux, mollement couchée, la tête appuyée sur la main et accoudée dans une *pose* décevante' [the seductive creature laid before his eyes, softly stretched out with her head leaning on one hand and leaning on her elbow in a deceptive *pose*] (*CH*, XI, 751, my emphasis), through her, Balzac turns his reader's attention to the sort of seductive 'performance' a man expects of a young woman (and of the deceptive stances the woman might consequently adopt). Similarly, in another tableau, Minna is represented as an ideal working-class young woman, dutifully bent over her sewing; she is also performing a role expected of her.[97] Likewise, we can read Wilfrid's various shows of violent emotion (striking the table in anger, turning away to hide his tears, making as though to throw himself off a cliff) as performances; like an actor on the stage, Wilfrid is there to act out those stormy feelings, to convey in an exaggerated, staged way the torments and desires which agitate a young man in love. The novel borrows from Balzac's relationship with Éveline, in that it is constructed almost entirely on the same dynamics of role-playing as is their correspondence; it highlights, and indeed exaggerates, the ways in which we perform different roles and 'selves' to different people (and it suggests how we can turn this ability to our advantage).

Already in his initial description of this novel Balzac shows that Séraphîtüs-Séraphîta is to possess knowledge which she will reveal to the other characters only gradually, and by the end she will have staged a theatrical 'happy ending': the couple finally understand their destiny and are united, accepting the earthly struggles to come, knowing that they will support each other. Balzac's description of Séraphîtüs-Séraphîta to Madame Hanska runs thus: 'il est aimé par un homme et par une femme, auxquels *il dit* [...] qu'ils ont aimé l'un et l'autre, l'amour qui les liait, en le voyant en lui, ange tout pur, et *il leur révèle* leur passion' [he is loved by a man and a woman, whom *he tells* [...] that they loved one another, the love that linked them, they had seen in him, a pure angel, and *he reveals* their passion to them].[98] Séraphîta's role seems to be to educate and enlighten the other characters as to their potential to adopt certain roles and leave behind their previous selves.

There is a general view in critical studies on *Séraphîta* that this novel was written for Madame Hanska's edification, more specifically to teach her about Swedenborgian doctrine.[99] Unfortunately, this has led to the novel being dismissed as of only limited relevance to the rest of the *Comédie humaine*. Critics have certainly been put off by the novel's skewed retellings of Swedenborg's theories.[100] I would argue, however, that it is not so much the doctrine of Swedenborg per se that Balzac wanted Éveline to absorb, but rather the idea (which he derives from Swedenborg but then manipulates to his own ends) of the potential for change inherent in the human self. Through *Séraphîta*, Balzac tried to show that new beginnings, rebirths, and remakings are possible, and that it is possible to 'rebecome' a former self and reclaim an earlier sense of identity.

Not only are the characters constantly evolving and changing (and, as Owen Heathcote suggests, we can even see this novel as containing the beginnings of future Balzac stories), but the very imagery used manages to subvert notions of beginnings and endings.[101] The dying Séraphîta, bowing her head, is described as a 'fleur trop chargée de rosée qui montre une dernière fois son calice et livre aux airs ses derniers parfums' [flower too weighed down by dew, showing its chalice for one last time, and filling the air with the last of its fragrance] (*CH*, XI, 841). Yet the flower charged with dew is a morning image, and therefore the death image here is curiously inverted. The novel even ends with a beginning, the image of the man and woman setting out on the path of life together, recalling Adam and Eve,[102] and looks outwards to a future: 'Au dehors, éclatait dans sa magnificence le premier été du dix-neuvième siècle' [Outside, the first summer of the nineteenth century was breaking out in all its splendour] (*CH*, XI, 860).

This open-endedness to the novel, which refuses to 'close' even as we arrive at its closing pages, may help explain why *Séraphîta* has for so long evaded a definitive interpretation. Balzac notes in his *Avant-Propos* to *La Comédie humaine* that he intended *Séraphîta* as a comment about the potential of man to be changeable, to remain 'indefinite'. He writes:

> Je crois aux progrès de l'homme sur lui-même. Ceux qui veulent apercevoir chez moi l'intention de considérer l'homme comme une créature finie se trompent donc étrangement. *Séraphîta*, la doctrine en action du Bouddha chrétien, me semble une réponse suffisante à cette accusation. (*CH*, I, 16)

[I believe in the progress of man's own development. Those who want to believe that I intended man to be considered as a finished creature are thus strangely mistaken. *Séraphîta*, which is the doctrine of the Christian Buddha in action, seems to me a sufficient response to this accusation.]

If Balzac is guilty of twisting the doctrines of Swedenborg, this is because he is using Swedenborg to his own ends — which include the seduction of Madame Hanska. In creating *Séraphîta* and pointing it out to Éveline as a model for their love, Balzac is essentially giving her a narrative in which there is a quasi-theological justification for their love affair.[103] The 'Buddhist' aspects of the novel,[104] notably the notion of rebirth and reincarnation, help Balzac suggest that it is in no way wrong to consider a completely fresh start, and to treat a new love affair as a completely new beginning, untainted by any past history, as Balzac did in his letters when he wrote 'car je suis né en 7bre 1833' [for I was born in September 1833], and when he addressed Éveline as though she were a virgin.[105] The theatrical discourse of performance and of 'rebecoming' which pervades Balzac's letters to Éveline — especially the earliest letters — culminates in the writing of this novel, which invites its reader, and specifically its *dédicataire,* Éveline Hanska, to open up to the possibility of a new life.

This chapter has shown how the undercurrents of performance in Balzac's letters to Hanska aim to persuade her of the acceptability of their relationship. As we have seen, Balzac adopts a series of roles designed to seduce Madame Hanska in different ways: child, lover, husband, even a sort of female confidante. His roles are not played out consistently over a period of time; Balzac can adopt several of them within the confines of a single letter. Each letter can be seen as a separate and deliberate performance, intended by turns to persuade, convince, and entertain. Indeed, some of them can be seen on close reading as carefully scripted mini–plays divided into 'scenes' that attempt to take their audience on a pre-planned emotional journey. Furthermore, Éveline is accorded a flattering role within each of these 'pieces,' or invited to see herself in the corresponding role, wife to Balzac's husband, mother to his son, lover to lover.

At the same time, she is credited with a great deal of creative control, with Balzac visibly shaping her in his own image as an all-powerful creator. When Balzac writes to Éveline in 1833 'je suis, je tâche d'être toi' [I am, I strive to be you], insinuating that he tries to imitate her and please her, this remark needs to be read in the context of other such remarks in the correspondence.[106] In 1834, while in Geneva, he writes, 'Non, tu es mon propre cœur. [...] Tu es un moi plus beau, plus gentil. [...] Tu es réellement moi-même' [No, you are my own heart. You are a more beautiful, kinder me. You are truly myself].[107] We note a slight change of dynamic, in that he seems to shift from writing about himself to focusing on her, ostensibly viewing Éveline as a better version of himself. Just before his departure from Vienna in June 1835, he writes a letter in which the two of them are an inseparable 'nous' [us].[108] In February 1846, Balzac describes himself as 'Noré qui t'adore et t'aime et te vénère comme un égoïste se vénère et s'adore lui-même' [Noré who adores and loves you and venerates you as a selfish man venerates and loves himself].[109] This comment recalls the 'définition de l'amour' which Balzac presents in *Le Médecin de campagne,* where he describes love as an 'égoïsme à deux. Nous nous aimons nous-mêmes en *l'autre*' [double egoism. It is ourselves we love in the *other*] (*CH*, IX, 562). We note that by this stage he has also written new 'stage names' for himself and Éveline — Noré and Line — which, each being a half of their original names, add up to a 'whole', thus underscoring Balzac's discourse of the 'one self'. In December 1846, Balzac adds, 'je ne suis qu'une modification de ton être' [I am but a modification of your being].[110] By 1847, he insists that it is Éveline who wields the creative power over him, and who has effectively been in charge of any 'modifications':

> Si je ne t'aimais pas à l'adoration, il y a longtemps que je n'existerais plus. Sans toi, je n'aurais [pas] survécu [...]. *Je suis ton ouvrage*, depuis *La Comédie humaine* jusqu'au souffle d'air qui entre dans mes poumons! [...] Je ne fais rien que pour toi, par toi, je n'ai plus d'existence propre.[111]

> [If I did not love you to the point of adoration, I would have ceased to exist a long time ago. Without you, I would not have survived [...]. *I am your creation*, from *La Comédie humaine* to the very breath that fills my lungs! [...] Everything I do is for you, I have no independent existence.]

Borrowing, and reappropriating, the famous remark of the marquise de Merteuil in *Les Liaisons dangereuses* — 'Je suis ton ouvrage' [I am your creation] — Balzac purportedly reinforces Éveline's supposed status as an all-powerful creator; yet the suggestion that she has the power to shape him is in fact a conceit, for in being shaped as a powerful creator she is only a projection of himself.[112] In the light of this, we can read Balzac's much-quoted maxim 'Lire, c'est créer peut-être à deux' [To read is to create, perhaps together] with a special focus on the ambiguous 'peut-être', as José-Luis Diaz suggests.[113] In ostensibly according to the Other the status of 'co-creator', Balzac by no means relinquishes his creative control.

The process of adopting roles in his correspondence holds another appeal for Balzac, namely the pleasure he appears to obtain from the possibilities of self-reinvention that are opened up within the 'performative space' of letter writing. In this sense, to use Brigitte Diaz's phrase previously cited, letters can function as 'brouillons de soi'. A correspondence permits inconsistency over time in the way that a novel, for example, with its requirements of internal coherence, cannot. Each letter is a finished article in itself, yet its meaning is continually redefined and nuanced by the letters that follow, and thus can never acquire a definitive, final meaning. The metaphor of each letter as a performance of the self is thus helpful, I think, in that it helps avoid the frustrations that the reader of letters can encounter at the constant contradictions that occur. No performance of a play is definitive; no letter is the definitive performance of the self.

In the next chapter, we will see in greater detail how Balzac's own re-reading of Madame Hanska's letters leads him to modify and overwrite his initial reactions to them. This aspect of Balzac as a re-reader adds a further dimension to the point that a correspondence, a continually evolving, growing, and morphing text, is never 'closed' or given a final or definite meaning, significance, or interpretation.

Notes to Chapter 2

1. *Corr*, I, 12–13. This imaginary conversation is reproduced by Laure Surville in her book about Balzac, but with inaccuracies; in her version, Balzac speaks of 'Moi-même' with a great deal of ill-humour (Surville, pp. 38–39).
2. On the theme of theatre in the letters to Madame Hanska, see: Nicole Mozet, '1848: Après "La Comédie humaine", le théâtre? Les Lettres à Mme Hanska comme paratexte', in *Paratextes balzaciens*, ed. by Le Huenen & Oliver, pp. 169–78; and Owen Heathcote, 'Balzac Between Work and Play: *Les Comédiens sans le savoir*', *Nottingham French Studies*, 51 (2012), 136–46.
3. Richard Schechner, *Essays on Performance Theory, 1970–1976* (New York: Drama Book Specialists, 1977), p. 2.
4. See Richard Schechner, *Performance Studies: An Introduction*, 2nd edn (New York & London: Routledge, 2006), p. 46.
5. See Schechner, *Essays*, p. 2.
6. See for instance *LMH*, I, 586–87 (9 June 1842), where Balzac begs Éveline to agree that they 'are' still in 1833.
7. Richard Schechner, *Between Theatre and Anthropology* (Philadelphia: University of Pennsylvania Press, 1985), p. 38.
8. *LMH*, I, 187 (25 August 1834).
9. *LMH*, I, 21 (January 1833).
10. *LMH*, I, 50 (19 August 1833). See also *LMH*, I, 210 (26 November 1834).
11. *LMH*, I, 189 (16 September 1834).
12. *LMH*, I, 189 (16 September 1834).
13. Ibid.
14. See Surville, p. LXXVI. This point is also made by Janet Sahli, 'Le Rôle de l'enfance dans *La Comédie humaine*', *L'Année balzacienne* (1975), 279–88 (p. 283).
15. This letter is cited in Stefan Zweig, *Balzac*, trans. by William and Dorothy Rose, 2nd edn (London: Cassell, 1970), pp. 207–08; also in Pierrot, *Honoré de Balzac*, pp. 228–29.
16. This is pointed out by Jeannine Guichardet, *Balzac mosaïque* (Clermont-Ferrand: Presses Universitaires Blaise Pascal, 2007), pp. 26–27.
17. *LMH*, I, 210 (26 November 1834). See also Guichardet, *Balzac mosaïque*, pp. 24–26.
18. *LMH*, I, 148 (11 March 1834).
19. *LMH*, I, 82 (31 October 1833).
20. *LMH*, I, 147 (11 March 1834).
21. *LMH*, I, 901 (11 August 1844).
22. *LMH*, I, 812 (20 February 1844).
23. *LMH*, I, 66 67 (18 October 1833).
24. See *Corr*, I, 876.
25. Robb, p. 244.
26. *LMH*, II, 1010 (28 September 1848).
27. This point is made by Sahli, p. 279.
28. For a more detailed analysis of this novel, see my article 'An Aesthetics of Indirection in Novels and Letters', pp. 229–46.
29. Bui uses the phrase '[un] être en devenir'. See Véronique Bui, *La Femme, la faute et l'écrivain: la mort féminine dans l'œuvre de Balzac* (Paris: Champion, 2003), p. 288.
30. Ibid..
31. *LMH*, I, 522 (16 December 1840).
32. There is something of this dynamic in the triangular relationship of Balzac, Éveline, and Anna, especially at a later stage of the correspondence when the grown-up Anna becomes something of an obstacle to Balzac's dream of marrying Éveline, who needs to see her daughter settled before she can contemplate her own future with Balzac. As Anna becomes more of a companion to her mother, Balzac finds himself competing for her attention. I return to this idea briefly in the next chapter.
33. Timothy Dobson, 'Aspects of the Mother and Child Relationship in Selected Novels of Honoré de Balzac and George Sand', (unpublished doctoral thesis, University of Manchester, 1990), pp.

27–28. In Balzac's *Le Curé de village* (1839), Véronique Graslin affirms that 'Nos œuvres, à nous, c'est nos enfants! Nos enfants sont nos tableaux, nos livres, nos statues' [Our works are our children! They are our paintings, our books, our statues] (*CH*, IX, 692).

34. Balzac's phonetic transcription of this Russian word, meaning 'serf', varies throughout the correspondence.

35. *LMH*, I, 112 (January 1834).

36. *LMH*, I, 193–94 (18 October 1834). See also other instances where Balzac refers to his enjoyment of this word: *LMH*, I, 159 (28 April 1834); *LMH*, I, 213 (15 December 1834); and especially *LMH*, I, 156 (10 April 1834).

37. *LMH*, I, 247 (May 1835).

38. *LMH*, I, 156 (10 April 1834).

39. *LMH*, I, 226 (16 January 1835).

40. *LMH*, I, 266 (11 August 1835).

41. *LMH*, I, 295 (30 January 1836).

42. See Zweig, p. 310. More recent biographers, for example Robb and Pierrot, mention Balzac's self-appellation as 'mougick' only in passing, and do not engage in any analysis of the *mougick* figure as a literary device (see Pierrot, *Balzac*, p. 247, and Robb, p. 228).

43. *LMH*, I, 173 (13 July 1834).

44. See Jean Starobinski, *Portrait de l'artiste en saltimbanque* (Paris: Gallimard, 2004, repr. 2013).

45. For examples of *bouffons* in nineteenth-century literature, as well as Balzac's famous reference to the 'bouffon' in *La Peau de chagrin* (cited at the start of this chapter, and echoed in *La Fille aux yeux d'or*, *CH*, V, 1097), we can find other 'bouffons' in Hugo's *Le Roi s'amuse* and Stendhal's *La Chartreuse de Parme*.

46. *Corr*, II, 392 (12 October 1833). See also *LMH*, I, 59, footnote 2.

47. See *LMH*, I, 62 (6 October 1833), and *LMH*, I, 61 (6 October 1833). See also *LMH*, I, 140 (21 February 1834), where the word 'épouse', meaning bride or spouse, has a clearly sexual connotation in the context in which it is used.

48. *LMH*, I, 104 (1 December 1833). In French, 'Ce que Dieu a uni, que l'homme ne le sépare pas' [That which God has united, let no man separate] is the relevant phrase from a traditional Christian marriage service. See also *LMH*, II, 621 (10 July 1847).

49. *LMH*, I, 53 (end of August 1833).

50. *LMH*, I, 114 (January 1834).

51. I paraphrase Schechner: see *Between Theatre and Anthropology*, p. 38.

52. *LMH*, I, 61 (6 October 1833).

53. 'Adoremus in aeternum, mon Éva, c'est notre devise, n'est-ce pas' [*Adoremus in aeternum*, that is our motto, my Eva, is it not] (*LMH*, I, 95, 17 November 1833).

54. See *CH*, V, 1036. It appears in the 1834 *La Duchesse de Langeais*, a novel which drew on Balzac's relationship with de Castries and was written before the relationship with Hanska began.

55. *LMH*, I, 90 (13 November 1833).

56. *LMH*, I, 92 (13 November 1833). Only briefly does Balzac recognize the impracticalities of the project once the cross is finished: 'Tu me diras ce que tu penses de la croix d'Anna. Nous avons été dominés par les cailloux, qui empêchaient de faire q[ue]lq[ue] chose de joli' [You will tell me what you think of Anna's cross. We have been dominated by pebbles, which prevented us from making something pretty of it] (*LMH*, I, 94, 17 November 1833).

57. 'The only way of expressing emotion in the form of art is by finding an "objective correlative"; in other words, a set of objects, a situation, a chain of events which shall be the formula of that *particular* emotion; such that when the external facts, which must terminate in sensory experience, are given, the emotion is immediately evoked,' T. S Eliot, 'Hamlet', in *Selected Essays* (London: Faber, 1972), pp. 141–46 (p. 145). Tim Farrant demonstrates how, in Balzac's fiction, painting imagery functions as a kind of 'objective correlative', see 'Balzac: du pittoresque au pictural', *L'Année balzacienne* (2004), 113–35 (pp. 132–33).

58. *LMH*, I, 210 (26 November 1834).

59. *LMH*, II, 503 (1 January 1847).

60. *LMH*, I, 634 (20 January 1843); *LMH*, II, 503 (1 January 1847); *LMH*, I, 173 (13 July 1834); ibid.

61. See Paul Jarry, *Le Dernier logis de Balzac, rue Fortunée, etc.* (Paris: Kra, 1924).

62. See *LMH*, I, 195 (18 October 1834).

63. *LMH*, I, 141–42 (22 February 1834).

64. *LMH*, I, 29 (24 February 1833).

65. *LMH*, II, 28 (26 February 1845). I will return to this extract in Chapter 3, where I discuss Balzac's 'collections' of objects.

66. *LMH*, I, 795 (28 January 1844). The colour violet recurs in sumptuous interiors in *La Comédie humaine*. See, for example, 'la chambre en violet' in *Une fille d'Ève*, (*CH*, II, 315), and a similar room in *César Birotteau* (*CH*, VI, 217).

67. *LMH*, I, 84 (3 November 1833).

68. *LMH*, I, 142 (22 February 1834).

69. Jeannine Guichardet, 'Honorine ou la fleur de son secret', in *Jardins et intimité dans la littérature européenne (1750–1920): actes du colloque du Centre de recherches révolutionnaires et romantiques, Université Blaise-Pascal, Clermont-Ferrand, 22–24 mars 2006*, ed. by Simone Bernard-Griffiths and others (Clermont-Ferrand: Presses Universitaires Blaise-Pascal, 2008), pp. 185–95 (pp. 190–91).

70. In this novella, where all the main characters are playacting in bad faith, interestingly enough the seducer would appear to be the least despicable member of the cast. Octave plays the devoted husband, and purports to have no idea what he did wrong (betraying himself when he wonders whether acting out the horrific denouement of Richardson's *Clarissa* — that is to say, raping Honorine, and thereby forcing her to have his child — would not suffice to win her back). Maurice de l'Hostal puts his early acting ambitions in the service of Octave's conjugal violence; and Honorine, returning to her much-hated husband, thus rebecomes a 'comédienne' for the worst reasons (*CH*, II, p. 570). For an analysis of the theme of marital rape in *Honorine*, see Diana Knight, 'Balzac's Honorine, or, The Rape of the Independent Woman', in *Women, Genre and Circumstance: Essays in Memory of Elizabeth Fallaize*, ed. by Margaret Atack and others (Oxford: Legenda, 2012), pp. 60–73.

71. *LMH*, I, 255–56 (28 June 1835).

72. *LMH*, I, 142 (22 February 1834).

73. *LMH*, I, 136 (15 February 1834). On Balzac's fetishization of his manuscripts, see Vachon, 'Un manuscrit dans une robe', in *Balzac: une poétique du roman*, pp. 321–29.

74. *LMH*, I, 645 (1 February 1843).

75. See *LMH*, I, 5–6.

76. *LMH*, I, 14 (7 November 1832).

77. *LMH*, I, 31 (March 1833).

78. *LMH*, I, 30 (end of March 1833).

79. *LMH*, I, 15 (7 November 1832).

80. *LMH*, I, 21 (end of January 1833).

81. *LMH*, I, 15 (7 November 1832).

82. *LMH*, I, 54 (9 September 1833).

83. *LMH*, I, 37 (29 May 1833).

84. *LMH*, I, 135 (15 February 1834).

85. *LMH*, I, 61 (6 October 1833).

86. *LMH*, I, 64 (13 October 1833).

87. *LMH*, I, 124 (24 January 1834).

88. *LMH*, I, 142 (22 February 1834).

89. See *CH*, XI, 727. The dedication opens with the words 'Madame, voici l'œuvre que vous m'avez demandée' [Madame, here is the work you have asked of me].

90. See *LMH*, I, 98 (20 November 1833).

91. Balzac, *Pensées, sujets, fragments*, p. 50. Cited in *LMH*, I, 98, n. 3.

92. Anne-Marie Baron, *Balzac occulte: alchimie, magnétisme, sociétés secrètes* (Lausanne: L'Age d'Homme, 2012), p. 228.

93. See for example *CH*, XI, 737, 747, & 753. Minna is aware that, when she is with Séraphîta, her thoughts and her words become altered. It is as though Séraphîta, like a prompter (*souffleur*) in the theatre, is able to prompt and influence the other two to speak exactly as she would wish them to.

94. See Juliette Frølich, 'L'Ange au pays des neiges: *Séraphîta*', *L'Année balzacienne* (1992), 319–31 (p. 322).

95. Joan Dargan, *Balzac and the Drama of Perspective: The Narrator in Selected Works of 'La Comédie humaine'* (Lexington, KY: French Forum, 1985), p. 159.

96. This question is posed by Henri Gauthier, 'Introduction', *CH*, XI, 720.

97. For an analysis of the motif of sewing in *La Comédie humaine*, and its link to role-playing and dissimulation, see my article 'An Aesthetics of Indirection in Novels and Letters', pp. 239–40.

98. *LMH*, I, 98 (20 November 1833), my emphasis.

99. See, for example, Hunt, p. 52.

100. Philosophers have denounced the absurdity of the ideology which frames the novel. See Saori Osuga, *Séraphîta et la Bible: sources scripturaires du mysticisme balzacien* (Paris: Champion, 2012), p. 19. Osuga provides an extensive overview of the criticisms aimed at *Séraphîta* by Swedenborgians and by Balzac's contemporaries. Henri Gauthier offers another possible explanation for Balzac's decision to use the doctrine of Swedenborg, albeit clumsily, in this novel; Gauthier suggests that it was in order to persuade an incredulous public to take his novel seriously. See 'Introduction', *CH*, XI, 702. For Anne-Marie Baron's recent study of Swedenborgian influences in this novel, see her study of *Séraphîta* in *Balzac occulte*, pp. 225–70 (especially pp. 232–41).

101. See Owen Heathcote, 'Spectres de Balzac? Personnage(s) reparaissant(s) et textes préexistants dans *Séraphîta*', *Eidôlon*, 52 (1999), 121–34.

102. This is pointed out by Baron, *Balzac occulte*, p. 234. Balzac's implicit allusion to Adam and Eve in *Séraphîta* recalls his use of the name 'Eve', and the concept of the 'first woman', in his seduction of Madame Hanska.

103. In his letters, Balzac invokes this novel to persuade, convince, and put at ease, the reluctant Éveline. The full quotation (already cited in part) reads: 'Allons, mon noble compagnon, ma chère Ève, jamais de doutes, vous me l'avez promis. Aimez avec confiance, *Séraphîta*, c'est nous deux, déployons donc nos ailes par un seul et même mouvement, aimons de la même manière. Je t'adore sans voir ni avant [*sic*], ni en arrière' [Come now, my noble companion, my dear Eve, no more doubts, you promised. Love me without fear, *Séraphîta* is the two of us, let us spread our wings using one and the same movement, let us love in the same way. I adore you without looking either forwards, or back] (*LMH*, I, 142, 22 February 1834).

104. Saori Osuga suggests that the ideas expressed in *Séraphîta* have a particularly strong resonance for a Buddhist reader. See *Séraphîta et la Bible*, 'Introduction', pp. 17–18.

105. *LMH*, II, 503 (1 January 1847).

106. *LMH*, I, 85 (6 November 1833).

107. *LMH*, I, 114–15 (January 1834).

108. 'Je n'ai pas d'âme assez étroite pour distinguer ce qui est à toi de ce qui est à moi, tout est à nous, cœur, âme, corps, sentiments, tout' [I am not so petty that I distinguish between what is yours and what is mine, everything is ours, heart, body, soul, sentiment, everything] (*LMH*, I, 250, June 1835).

109. *LMH*, II, 183 (18 February 1846).

110. *LMH*, II, 478 (20 December 1846).

111. *LMH*, II, 551 (15 May 1847), my emphasis.

112. In Letter 81, the marquise de Merteuil boasts to Valmont: 'Je puis dire que suis mon ouvrage' [I can say that I am my own creation]. See Pierre Choderlos de Laclos, *Les Liaisons dangereuses* (Paris: Flammarion, 1981), p. 172.

113. See José-Luis Diaz, ' "Créer peut-être à deux" ', p. 40.

CHAPTER 3

❖

Balzac Collector, Rereader, and Storyteller

A force de contempler les objets qui m'entouraient, je trouvais à chacun sa physionomie, son caractère; souvent ils me parlaient: si, par-dessus les toits, le soleil couchant jetait à travers mon étroite fenêtre quelque lueur furtive, ils se coloraient, pâlissaient, brillaient, s'attristaient ou s'égayaient.

[From gazing so much at the objects that surrounded me, I ended up endowing each one with its own physiognomy, its character; often, they spoke to me: whenever the rays of the setting sun furtively made an entrance through my narrow window, these objects would burst into colour, grow pale, glitter, become sad or joyous.]

BALZAC, *La Peau de chagrin* (*CH*, x, 138)

Puis, je l'avoue à ma honte, je ne conçois pas l'amour dans la misère. [...] J'aime à froisser sous mes désirs de pimpantes toilettes, à briser des fleurs, à porter une main dévastatrice dans les élégants édifices d'une coiffure embaumée.

[Also, I am ashamed to admit, I cannot imagine love amid poverty. [...] I like to crumple an elegant dress as I wish, to break flowers, to run a devastating hand through the carefully-constructed edifice of a fragrant coiffure.]

BALZAC, *La Peau de chagrin* (*CH*, x, 142)

Balzac's well-documented passion for objects translates itself, particularly in his later life, into a passion for collecting. His 'bricabracomanie' [bricabracomania], to use his own word,[1] is especially evident in his later letters to Madame Hanska, most notably those from 1845 onwards, in which he describes his latest acquisitions, refuting her objections to his careless spending, and boasting of his successes in his 'royaume de Bricabracquie' [kingdom of Bric-a-Brac-land].[2]

Throughout his life, Balzac enjoyed purchasing interesting objects at a bargain price. We know from his early correspondence that his first acquisitions for his attic room in the rue de Lesdiguières were a mirror and a picture — an extravagance which earned him a reprimand from his family, and which attests, very early on, to his liking for decorative (and superfluous) objects for the home.[3]

In the light of Balzac's passion for collecting, this chapter proposes a study of the ways in which his correspondence with Madame Hanska functions as a treasured collection, of memories, of sensory impressions, and as a collection of objects in themselves. Balzac's collection is continually given new life by his continued rereadings of the letters, which fuel his creative imagination. No study has been undertaken to date of Balzac as a rereader; yet, as my analysis will show, Balzac's processes of rereading are a vital prelude to the processes of storytelling and creation. The writer's relationship to objects, including letters, and his tendency continually to reimagine them, reinterpret them, and weave new narratives around them, is central to his process of artistic creation. It is not so much that the objects are treasured merely for their own sake; rather, their value to Balzac comes from their capacity to help him generate ideas that can find expression in words.

In the *Avant-propos* (1842) to *La Comédie humaine*, Balzac states that it is 'les hommes, les femmes et *les choses*' [men, women and *things*] (*CH*, I, 9, my emphasis) which form the subject of his *œuvre*; for Balzac, the object has a representative function, and 'speaks' for its owner.[4] It is not surprising, in view of his passion for collecting things, that he should make the collection into a key theme in one of his novels; Emma Bielecki suggests that he was the first French novelist to do this.[5] It is in *Le Cousin Pons* (1847) that the theme appears most obviously; however, some of Balzac's earlier novels also feature the practice of collecting. As Hunt has pointed out, Balzac had 'sprinkled' the pages of *La Comédie humaine* with many references to works of art, such as later form part of Pons's collection.[6] Characters who practice collecting within *La Comédie humaine* include M. de Watteville in *Albert Savarus*, whose fancy for collecting small valueless objects Balzac equates with the early stages of madness (*CH*, I, 914).[7] In *La Muse du département* (1843), the heroine's attempts at collecting are represented as a somewhat futile pursuit, through which she attempts to fill a fundamental void, and to represent herself as a cultured woman (yet managing only to come across as a pretentious provincial). The collection of Dinah de la Baudraye is linked to her disappointment, loneliness, and lack of fulfillment.[8] In *Honorine*, as Tim Farrant points out, instances of what we might term 'collecting', on both the part of Octave and Honorine, 'point to a forlorn desire to fix the transient, to reify life'.[9] As we shall see, similarly melancholy resonances can be found in Balzac's allusions to his collecting practices in the letters to Madame Hanska, and might be interpreted as being suggestive of a kind of mourning for a former time; however, as we shall also see in the course of this chapter, this potentially negative aspect of collecting is one which Balzac subverts in order to derive from it both pleasure and creativity.

Le Cousin Pons, written at the height of Balzac's collecting 'addiction', famously describes the collection of objets d'art as 'l'héroïne de cette histoire' [the heroine of this story] (CH, VII, 763). In representing it thus, Balzac not only gives the collection centre-stage in this work, but also personifies and indeed eroticizes it. Pons, its owner, is described like a lover, his feelings towards his collection equated to 'l'amour de l'amant pour une belle maîtresse' [a lover's love for a beautiful mistress] (CH, VII, 491).[10] For Balzac, then, a collection can have an emotional or erotic dimension, similar to that invested by artists in their creations (for example by male characters such as Frenhofer, as discussed in Chapter 2). Balzac suggests that collections, too, can fill a lack, and become an object of desire onto which, in the absence of another love object, fantasies can be projected.

This sublimation of desires is in evidence in Balzac's later letters to Madame Hanska; in her continued absence, his growing obsession with collecting valuable objects hints at the need to fill a similar void. Balzac's triumphant collecting is detailed in his letters alongside episodes of deep melancholia, suggesting that, as he says, the processes of collecting are perhaps a protection, a distraction from the pressing concerns of his own mortality and fragility, and the uncertainty of his relationship with Éveline. Whereas Chapter 2 revealed how the earlier letters of Balzac to Éveline show him confidently weaving the story of their love affair, in later years Balzac's letters show him turning to collecting in order to cope with her continued absence.

Balzac's correspondence with Éveline records the different categories of 'collections' which attract him over the course of their relationship. With his magpie-like propensity for beautiful things, Balzac set in motion a process of exchange of objects (small gifts, tokens, flower petals), which continued throughout the relationship. As the correspondence unfolds, we can see how over the years he built up a 'collection' of these objects related to her, and how he treated this collection as almost a museum or shrine. In one letter, he suggested that the smallest gift — 'une paille' [a mere straw] — can become 'tout un musée pour le cœur' [a whole museum for the heart].[11] The apparently valueless gift can, in the memory of the giver, appear to be equal in value to a whole museum collection. The sending of small symbolic gifts is, in this regard, just as important as receiving them.

Whenever Balzac encloses flower petals in letters, behind the typical Romantic clichés such as 'La rose ce sont les baisers' [The rose stands for kisses], there is a strong undercurrent of sensuality; for example, as the correspondence progresses, Balzac links the flower petals more explicitly to kisses (he describes kissing them, or holding them between his lips).[12] In the gifts he sends out, and in the gifts he requests, we can discern overtones of the sensual and the sexual. Balzac's fantasy of being able to send her enough of his hair, for instance, 'pour que vous en eussiez des chaînes et des bracelets' [so that you could have chains and bracelets of it] is highly suggestive.[13] (Although the exchanging of locks of hair was a common Romantic gesture, we can discern a fetishistic preoccupation in Balzac's desire to cover Éveline's body with this excess of jewellery made out of his own hair.) Like the blank page which brought Balzac the idea of touching the correspondent's white arm, the desire for her to wear his hair on her body suggests a desire for a physical contact of sorts during their separation. As we saw in an earlier chapter in the example of the 'petite cassette' [little box] he had sent her, he clearly wants his gifts to be handled and touched.

The gifts which Balzac *demands* from her also carry an erotic charge. When, as we have seen, Balzac asks her for a 'bout de ruban blanc' [piece of white ribbon] in place of an unscented violet, it is significant that he should ask for a sensual gift which has been worn on the body.[14] This becomes something of a pattern: as we know, Balzac also asks for a piece of Éveline's grey dress for the binding of *Séraphîta*; another time, for a black rag, again from her dress, with which to wipe his pen. Thus Balzac's desire to collect objects from Éveline is deeply rooted in fetishistic tendencies, and is furthermore suggestive of his pent-up sexual desire which, during the early days of the correspondence in particular, he chooses not to verbalize, but which finds its expression in these exchanges of sensual gifts.[15]

Thus we can see that, from the earliest days of the correspondence, this exchange of small objects of sentimental value is part and parcel of the letter-exchange; the small tokens are a supplement to the words on the page, a sub-collection within the collection of letters. As the epistolary relationship progresses and more valuable objects are exchanged, Balzac comes to possess a veritable 'collection' of objects relating to Éveline. 'Enfin, c'est toi partout, matériellement parlant' [It's you everywhere, materially speaking], he writes in 1845.[16] In his letters, Balzac begins to dwell on those objects, and especially on his arrangement of them in his home. He describes viewing, re-admiring and re-experiencing them, as though they were indeed a sort of private museum. As Adrien Goetz has noted, the collector is marked by a propensity to arrange his collectables attractively, so that each item may appear to its best advantage when set alongside others.[17] Balzac displays precisely this propensity when he describes the following carefully arranged collection:

> Mes yeux ne peuvent rencontrer que le tapis-tartan qui couvre devant moi une table ronde; le Daffinger à ma droite, sur cette petite table où j'écris depuis 15 ans, les malachites, l'encrier-chien d'Anna. Sur le velours de la paroi, le paysage de W[ierzchownia]. A côté, l'encrier du voyage. Sur un petit meuble, la fameuse boîte, dont la sœur est à vous, et où sont les lettres, les mouchoirs, les reliques! Le portefeuille de Vienne. [...] Et si je regarde mon papier [...], l'annulaire de la main gauche a l'hyacinthe et l'alliance![18]

> [My eyes cannot help but find the tartan rug which covers the round table before me; the Daffinger on my right, on this little table from where I write to you for the past 15 years, the malachites, the dog-inkwell from Anna. On the velvet partition, the W[ierzchownia] landscape. Next to it, the travel inkwell. On a little piece of furniture, the famous box, whose sister is in your hands, and in it are the letters, handkerchiefs, relics! The wallet from Vienna. [...] And if I look down at my paper [...], the ring finger of the left hand has the hyacinth and the wedding band!]

This and other similar passages in which Balzac describes various beloved objects which he has set before him, all share an insistence on their arrangement; where they are in relation to him and to one another is carefully described, letting Madame Hanska know that these objects have been displayed with care. However, the insistence here is not only on the significance of the objects in themselves, but on the significance which Balzac accords to them *in relation to his writing*. This collection has been arranged on Balzac's writing table in such a way that all his souvenirs of Éveline can become associated with letter-writing — even objects such as pictures, which are not ostensibly linked to writing, but which, as we saw in an earlier chapter, can become a source of inspiration. 'Wierzchownia, le petit profil, Daffinger, voilà ce qui m'entoure, je cherche mes mots et mes corrections dans ces chers souvenirs' [Wierzchownia, the little profile, the Daffinger, this is what surrounds me, I look for my words and my corrections in these dear memories], he writes in 1844.[19] Thus the objects are 'témoignages' [tokens, or mementoes] not only of his relationship, but of his writing of letters and novels; the two — Balzac's relationship with Éveline and his writing process — are deliberately conflated. The shrine which purports to celebrate Éveline is in fact much more explicitly set up to be a celebration of Balzac's own creativity, thus reinforcing the idea that the objects are treasured above all for their contribution to Balzac's ability to generate language and stories.

From the small tokens sent to him in letters, Balzac progresses to collecting objects of value to his writing process. From here, he eventually moves on to collecting furniture, artworks, and bric-a-brac for his and Éveline's future Parisian home, and his drive to collect appears continuously to escalate. All of his grand purchases and special finds are minutely described in letters to her. This collection was intended to rival that of Wierzchownia, the opulent family home of Madame Hanska.[20] Balzac himself implied as much when he confided in her daughter Anna, 'Je veux que cette maison soit un écrin digne des bijoux qui y seront serrés, et qu'en venant des splendeurs de Wisnovitz, nos amours de Saltimbanques et *leurs enfants* ne soient pas dépaysés' [I want this house to be a worthy jewel-case for the jewels that shall be secured in there, and that in coming from the splendours of Wisnovitz, our enamoured Entertainers and *their children* shall not feel lost].[21] Yet I would also like to draw attention to Balzac's choice of the word 'écrin'. He insists several times in the correspondence on representing the house as a jewel-case, with Éveline as a pearl to be shut up within. He seems to objectify her even more concretely when he writes 'La petite fille sera dans son écrin comme doit y être une chose précieuse, un diamant sans pair, un bijou sans rival' [The little girl will be in her jewel-case like a precious thing ought to be, a diamond like no other, an unrivalled jewel].[22] 'La petite fille' was one of the portraits of Éveline in Balzac's possession; in this letter, the mistress and the small portrait become blurred into one, and she becomes an object which can be shut away, thus lending greater weight to Balzac's metaphor of the jewel-case and exposing the collector's jealous drive to possession.

Balzac's collection for the rue Fortunée serves several functions. In one letter he writes, 'J'amasse des meubles, comme l'oiseau des brins de paille. Ne me gronde pas, laisse-moi tromper l'attente par ces petits soins, par ces leurres' [I collect furniture like a bird collects wisps of straw. Do not scold me, let me conquer the wait by these little attentions, by these illusions].[23] Not only is Balzac building a 'nest', trying to attract a mate, but the drive to collect is part of his attempt to deceive time, to stop himself from feeling that he may be waiting for his lover forever. The practice of collecting is an illusion, a decoy, providing him with a sense of purpose and progress which makes this period in his life feel less empty. On another occasion, Balzac explains to Éveline that the discourse of collecting which runs through the letters is also part of his attempt to reduce 'l'effet de cette affreuse maladie de l'âme qui s'appelle *l'absence*' [the effect of this awful malady of the soul which is called *absence*]:[24]

> Je ne t'écrivais pas: *puissances du ciel!* etc., je te parlais affaires, chiffons, et je me mourais. Mon lplp. je serais mort sans phrases et sans exagération, la vie n'était plus ni au cœur, ni au cerveau, ni dans l'estomac [...], elle était absente, comme toi![25]

> [I was not writing you things like '*Dear God!*', I was telling you about business deals, finery, and I was dying. My [little wolf], I would be dead without words and without exaggeration, my life was no longer in my heart, nor in my brain or my stomach [...], it was absent, like you!]

Thus only rarely does Balzac admit that collecting, and writing about collecting, sometimes functions as a survival mechanism for coping with Éveline's absence, a displacement activity filled with the promise of her arrival (a promise which he, on some level, knows to be empty). Balzac here draws attention to the function of *writing*, and writing the collection, in attempting to hide from the inevitable fact that his efforts are all in the service of someone absent — for, clearly, Madame Hanska shows no urgent desire to join him in Paris, and Balzac is for the most part excluded from the pleasures she shares with her 'children', Anna and her husband Georges (whom Balzac, too, would like to 'collect'; if Éveline's beloved daughter and her husband were to come and live with Balzac, she could certainly be persuaded to follow).[26] It is not the collection itself which is important, but rather the phrases of Balzac's letters which communicate its existence to Éveline, and which help Balzac spin the fantasy of a richer, more carefree life with her.

The whole collection of the rue Fortunée, then, including the smaller-scale collections of treasured objects which relate to Madame Hanska, is constructed in the letters around its missing 'pearl' — that is to say, around a fundamental void or absence. 'Je commence à prendre en haine cette maison vide, où tout est fait pour une absente' [I am starting to hate this empty house, in which everything was made for an absent person], a discouraged Balzac writes in June 1847.[27] However, only very rarely do his letters focus on the notion of emptiness. Instead, Balzac tends to employ the discourse of the collection in order to help him focus on the literal and metaphorical riches to be gained from this relationship.

Une lettre! ne savez-vous pas que c'est un de mes trésors?[28]

[A letter! Do you not know that it is one of my treasures?]

The letters that Balzac sends to Éveline function for him as a place where he records his collecting practices, and where his thoughts and memories of her are likewise gathered and then sent to her. This section of my study now turns to his attitude towards the letters that he receives from Madame Hanska. Like the collections of objects discussed above, these letters, too, functioned first and foremost as a physical collection, since Balzac actively saved and kept them. (As we know, Balzac and his mistress eventually agreed to destroy the bulk of this collection of letters to avoid the possibility of blackmail, and Balzac's description of his despair at having to destroy his precious collection in itself reinforces its importance to him. His account of throwing the letters into the fire 'une à une regardant les dates' [one by one while looking at the dates], this meticulous recording of his catalogue of letters even as it is about to be destroyed, as well as his attempts to rescue any small tokens he can from this correspondence, emphasizes the status of the letters as a cherished physical collection.)[29]

Baron has noted Balzac's predilection for letters and writing paper.[30] As we saw in Chapter 1, Balzac fetishized the blank pages of paper sent to him by Éveline, describing how he kissed the white page which, by a kind of metonymy, comes to represent the woman's arm. The pages covered in Éveline's handwriting are fetishized too: 'Ta chère écriture me bouleverse; elle rayonne à mes yeux comme le soleil. Je te sens, te respire quand je la vois' [Your dear handwriting overwhelms me; it shines before my eyes like the sun. I can feel you, I breathe you in when I see it].[31] Here, Éveline's very handwriting metonymically evokes her. The cherished pages of her letters function as a fetish: they can be locked away, reread, touched, smelled, kissed, and worshipped. Indeed, somewhat poignantly, Balzac says that the 'seule volupté' [only delight] of the letter-writer 'c'est de n[ous] lire et de n[ous] relire' [is to read and reread one another], to be able to revisit and reread the letters from the absent lover.[32]

In *Le Cousin Pons*, as noted above, Pons's collection of precious objects is personified, in the sense that we are told of how Pons treats it as 'une belle maîtresse' [a beautiful mistress] and the narrator tells us that it is the heroine of the story (*CH*, VII, 491). In the same way, Balzac's collection of Éveline's letters also undergoes a sort of personification. When he describes putting her letters away in the 'joli coffret' [pretty coffer] which he had made for them, he describes treating them 'coquettishly', as though they were creatures: 'pour moi, vos lettres sont des créatures, des fées qui m'apportent mille délices; et je suis coquet pour mes lettres-fées' [to me your letters are creatures, fairies, which bring me a thousand delights; and I am coquettish with my letter-fairies].[33] The 'lettres-fées', treated as though they were alive, are talked to and communed with. Balzac's description of the letters as fairies is especially striking, because the fairy allusion recalls similar descriptions of Madame Hanska as 'fée' in the early correspondence.[34]

We remember also that in his early novel *La Dernière Fée*, Balzac portrayed a naïve young man whose dream of falling in love with a real-life fairy in a sense came true, as he found himself whisked away by a beautiful and fantastically wealthy woman — who is as close to a real-life 'fairy' as any woman might be. The link between this fantasy woman and Éveline, an aristocratic *Étrangère*, is not at all tenuous; when her letters, with their noble coat of arms and expensive postmark, first made their appearance, they very likely recalled to Balzac this fictional wealthy woman who appears as though from nowhere in response to a fervent wish. The idea of the letter-fairies, therefore, counts for more than a mere turn of phrase, and may have a deeper, and indeed erotic, fantasy dimension to it.

Furthermore, in Balzac's creative mind, the concept of the 'fairy' is also linked to his own private flights of inspiration and artistic *jouissance*. When he describes himself enjoying the finale of Beethoven's Symphony No. 5 in C Minor, he says the experience gives him access to 'des beautés d'un genre inconnu, les fées de la fantaisie, [...] des créatures qui voltigent avec les beautés de la femme et les ailes diaprées de l'ange' [beauties of an unknown kind, fairies of fantasy, [...] creatures who flit about, with a woman's beauty and an angel's rainbow wings].[35] From this passage, we can see that, to Balzac, the concept of 'fairies' has connotations of the ideal object of desire on the one hand, and the idea of artistic delight on the other. By association, the 'letter-fairies' are not only eroticized objects, but are also receptacles of his creative impulses.

Within Balzac's correspondence with Éveline, then, we can distinguish between different categories of collecting. First of all, the letters constitute a record of Balzac's collecting practices. Secondly, the letters are a physical collection of pieces of paper, which are enjoyed for their erotic associations, and for the additional meaning with which they can become imbued. Thirdly, and perhaps most importantly, the letters are a collection of memories, thoughts, and ideas.

Letters from the lover excite Balzac's senses. Like the sight of the 'pieds de mouche' [spidery scrawl] of her handwriting,[36] the fragrance which lingers on her writing paper is a tangible reminder of her.[37] The scent acts as a Proustian trigger *avant la lettre*, transporting Balzac back to memories of times spent together; it immediately evokes sensual memories of the correspondent, such as the sound of her voice, or the feel of her hand:

> Le parfum de votre papier qui ne s'exhale pas tout entier, [...] c'est un esquif chargé de souvenirs et qui me mène loin! [...] Je revois le sentier de Diodati ou les cailloux de l'allée du milieu du jardin de la maison Mirabaud où n[ous] n[ous] promenions, ou un certain accent, une certaine pression de mains presqu'enfantine en regardant des gravures.[38]

> [The scent of your letter-paper which does not fade entirely, [...] is a skiff weighed down with memories and which takes me far away! [...] I revisit the path to Diodati or the pebbles of the alley in the middle of the garden of the Mirabaud house where we had walked, or a certain accent, a certain almost childlike pressure of the hand while we were looking at etchings.]

The letters thus constitute a repository of memories; here, the letter evokes sensory 'correspondances', in a quasi-Baudelairian (and Swedenborgian) sense of the term.[39]

Balzac's own letters to Éveline reminisce over all things sensual — recalling, for example, the colour of her dress back on the day of their first meeting, and the sight of her face at the window, or the pebbles under his feet — in short, recalling the occasion of the first meeting in terms of specific sensory memories. In 1845, he claims that the names of all the places they have travelled to produce in him a sensation similar to that produced by music: 'Pour moi c'est quand l'un de ces noms vient dans ma pensée comme si un Chopin touchait une touche de piano; le marteau réveille des sons qui vibrent dans mon âme, et il s'éveille tout un long *poème*' [For me, when one of those names comes to my mind, it is as though a Chopin were pressing a key on the piano; the piano hammer arouses sounds which vibrate in my soul, and a whole long *poem* stirs and wakes].[40] Balzac's recollections of the places they have visited (recollections which he describes as a 'fragment of a poem'), take the form of a lyrical post-script to a letter where he pours out his recollections of times spent together.[41] In the letter of 12 December 1845, Balzac's lyrical evocation of the 'vingt-trois villes [...] sacrées' [twenty-three sacred cities] attempts to note down the associations contained for him within the names of each city to which they have travelled.[42] He attempts to do this through sustaining the musical metaphor of 'des sons qui vibrent dans mon âme'.[43] He writes, for example, that their reunion in St Petersburg was 'sans une note fausse' [without one false note]; 'le génie de Beethoven, [...] le sublime' [the genius of Beethoven, [...] the sublime] frames his memories of Passy and Fontainebleau; and Orléans, Bourges, Tours, and Blois were 'des *concertos*, des symphonies bien-aimées, [...] mais où la souffrance d'un *loup* jette des notes graves' [concertos, beloved symphonies, [...] yet with the suffering of a little wolf adding some low notes].[44] An even more telling and more evocative list of the visited cities is to be found in one of Balzac's manuscripts:

Neufchâtel [*sic*] (en Suisse): une lettre à la main; Genève: une clef; Vienne (Autriche): un doigt sur les lèvres; Pétersbourg: un doigt faisant signe de venir; Dresde: appuyée sur une viole; Cannstadt: [appuyée] sur un fauteuil; Carlsruhe: tenant un sablier; Strasbourg: coiffée d'un bonnet phrygien et tenant 2; Passy: une main sur les yeux; Fontainebleau: tenant un flambeau; Orléans: une boule d'or; Bourges: appuyée sur une roue; Tours: tenant trois amandes; Blois: [tenant] une poire; Paris: cinq couronnes à la main; Rotterdam: une torche renversée; La Haye: un cornet du Japon; Anvers: une coquille; Bruxelles: tenant six roses; Baden-Baden: couronnée de myosotis; Lyon: tenant une palme; Valence; Toulon; Naples.[45]

[Neufchâtel [*sic*] (in Switzerland): a letter in the hand; Geneva, a key; Vienna (Austria): a finger on the lips; Petersbourg: a finger beckoning; Dresden: leaning against a viol; Cannstadt: [leaning] on an armchair; Carlsruhe: holding an hourglass; Strasbourg: wearing a Phrygian hat and holding 2; Passy: a hand over the eyes; Fontainebleau: holding a torch; Orleans: a golden ball; Bourges: leaning on a wheel; Tours: holding three almonds; Blois: [holding] a pear; Paris: five crowns in the hand; Rotterdam: a torch knocked over; La Haye: a Japanese horn; Anvers: a sea shell; Brussels: holding six roses; Baden-Baden: crowned with forget-me-nots; Lyon, holding a palm; Valencia; Toulon; Naples.]

These collected memories of the cities visited together are all sensory, and most are visual. Sound, which at first glance seems absent from these demonstrably silent tableaux, is in fact there in the original French, incorporated into the musicality of the words — for example, in the couplets 'Fontainebleau: tenant un flambeau; Orléans: une boule d'or', or in 'Blois: [tenant] une poire ', the sounds of the place name are echoed in the sounds of the words which follow. The name of the place does indeed function as Balzac's metaphorical piano key, arousing certain sounds and associations. While the list of the place names is intimately connected to memories of Éveline, the evocations which follow each name are perhaps more likely to be of artworks, or sculptures, than of her. In listing these cities as a collection of images which have caught his attention, Balzac makes them into a gallery of memories, a collection of tableaux.

These sensory recollections provided by the letters are enjoyed by Balzac in Éveline's continued absence. While the collections of objects relating to her were described by Balzac as creating an 'atmosphère tuante' [deadly atmosphere], reminding him continually of her absence, the letters seem to help him evoke her with much greater immediacy.[46] Furthermore, unlike the other collections which seem to create a kind of sterility (as he implies with the above comment), Balzac's experience of returning to the letters fuels his own creativity and desire to write: 'Quand je relis ce que tu me dis de mes lettres, tu me donnes envie de t'écrire toujours' [When I reread what you tell me of my letters, you make me want to write to you forever].[47]

The reason for collecting and hoarding the letters is clearly the desire to be able to *reread* them; and it is the act of rereading the letters — the possibility of continually re-interrogating the text, of refusing to stop at the first reading and at the initial meaning — which saves the letter-collection from becoming mortiferous. There is a parallel between the idea of rereading and the activity of the collector. The collector of objects keeps them in order to look at and experience them over and over again, as a source of safe and repeated pleasure, as well as in order to find new aspects to explore or admire, much as Balzac does with Éveline's letters.

We have seen, then, that Balzac's collecting practices are a vital and recurrent theme in the *Lettres à Madame Hanska*, to the point where the letters themselves become an instance of this collecting habit, as well as a repository for ideas and images that Balzac wished to record. Rereading the letters can then be used to generate new interpretations and new texts. In particular, in the absence of new letters, rereading old letters of Éveline's can be used as a way for Balzac to generate new texts of his own, and this is suggestive in terms both of the way that Balzac relates to and uses objects in his storytelling, and in terms of his creative methods more generally.

Rereading: a treat, a form of escape, a device for getting to sleep or for dis-
tracting oneself, a way to evoke memories (not only of the text but of one's life
and of past selves), a reminder of half-forgotten truths, an inlet to new insight.
It rouses or soothes, provokes or reassures.[48]

Balzac's portrayal of himself as a rereader of letters is present in the correspondence
from a very early stage. In January 1833, he signs off a letter to Éveline by saying
'je galope vers la Pologne et je relis toutes vos lettres — je n'en ai que trois' [I
am galloping towards Poland and I reread all your letters — I only have three].[49]
This initial reaction to her letters — the desire to reread and re-experience the
frustratingly few letters he has, and the sense of eagerness and imaginary displacement
they inspire — already hints at the pleasures to be gained from rereading them. The
literary quality of Éveline's letters means that they lend themselves to rereading.
Balzac refers to them as literary masterpieces — 'Ce serait de ma meilleure copie!' [This
would be my very best work!][50] — and rereads them sometimes simply for distraction,
'Il n'y a pas de spectacles, et il n'y a rien à lire, j'ai relu tes lettres' [There are no plays
on, and there is nothing to read, I've reread your letters].[51] He further suggests that
the second reading is more important than the initial reading: 'Quand ces lettres
viennent, je les lis en homme pressé de causer avec vous, je ne les déguste qu'à une
seconde lecture, qui ne vient que capricieusement' [When these letters come, I read
them as someone impatient to talk to you; I only savour them upon the second
reading, which comes but capriciously].[52] Balzac here is discussing the first reading
in similar terms to Vladimir Nabokov, who suggested that the word 'reader' can
only be used loosely:

One cannot *read* a book: one can only reread it. [...] When we read a book for
the first time the very process of laboriously moving our eyes from left to right,
line after line, page after page, this complicated physical work upon the book,
the very process of learning in terms of space and time what the book is about,
this stands between us and artistic appreciation.[53]

When Balzac first reads a letter from Éveline, he is in a state of high excitement,
not conducive to savouring the letter, impatient as he is to enter into a dialogue.
Only later is he able to enjoy the letter as a literary artefact and a text in itself. As
with painting or literature, the full meaning of the letter cannot be apprehended
all at once.

If we compare the number of references to rereading in Balzac's *Correspondance*
and in his letters to Madame Hanska, we see that the latter are far more numerous;
Balzac talks about rereading much more often in his letters to Éveline.[54] Compared
to his other correspondents, her letters are rarer, come from a more exotic location,
and seem to mean more to him on a personal level. Balzac clearly considered
rereading to be important in general, and this idea is reflected in *La Comédie
humaine*. In his 'Préface' to *Une fille d'Ève* (1839), he described how, through the
device of recurring characters, he planned to compel his readers to reread.[55] He
suggests explicitly that he aimed to turn *La Comédie humaine* into 'une œuvre digne

d'être relue' [a work worthy of being reread], and to incite his reader to undertake a 'seconde lecture' [second reading] (*CH*, II, 266), by forcing him or her to revisit the characters' stories in a surprising and often non-linear fashion:

> Vous trouverez, par exemple, l'actrice Florine peinte au milieu de sa vie, dans *Une fille d'Ève*, Scène de la vie privée, et vous la verrez à son début dans *Illusions perdues*, Scène de la vie de province. [...] Enfin, vous aurez le milieu d'une vie avant son commencement, le commencement après sa fin, l'histoire de la mort avant celle de la naissance. (*CH*, II, 264–65)[56]

> [You shall find Florine the actress, for example, painted in the middle of her life in *Une fille d'Ève*, Scène de la vie privée, and you will see her beginnings in *Illusions perdues*, Scène de la vie de province. [...] You will have the middle part of a life before its beginnings, the beginnings after the end, the story of someone's death before that of their birth.]

Not only did the device of recurring characters allow Balzac the possibility of continually rewriting, adapting, sometimes completely changing his characters' stories (we can think, for example, of the dubious transformation of Félix de Vandenesse; the clear-headed, capable and somewhat humourless adult of *Une fille d'Ève* seems an unlikely candidate for a childhood such as was ascribed to the sensitive protagonist of *Le Lys dans la vallée*).[57] Jeannine Guichardet suggests that Balzac sees so many possible beginnings (*amorces*) of stories that he does not want to have to be confined to only one life story per character.[58] Yet there is in fact more at stake here than just the opportunity for gratuitous reinvention; for can we not in fact view Balzac's celebrated literary device as a way to avoid, rather than encourage, rereading? In re-encountering previously familiar figures in new Balzac novels, his readers are indeed undertaking a 'second reading' of a story — an engineered 'second reading' of sorts; built in to the very fabric of the *œuvre*, it has been inconspicuously provided by the author himself. Balzac's readers find themselves forced to reinterrogate, in their minds, familiar stories when reading new ones, and to readjust ideas they may have formed earlier. Balzac's highly ambiguous comment on inciting the 'seconde lecture' does not necessarily mean that he actually hoped 'to spur his readers on to explore more' of their own accord.[59] Rather, it would seem that 'cette admirable invention de Balzac', as Proust described the device of recurring characters, provides a carefully directed rereading, one which forcibly overrides and partially obscures earlier ones.[60]

Balzac's characters themselves also read and reread, be it novels or especially letters, which they reread most frequently. This is generally alluded to only in passing; perhaps partly for this reason, their rereadings have gone largely unnoticed by scholars.[61] Balzac's novels portray several types of rereadings. The childish pleasure of rereading a favourite text (in this case, a story, rather than a letter) appears in Balzac's work as early as 1823, in *La Dernière Fée,* a precursor to many of the themes of Balzac's later fiction (we remember that it was in the opening of this novel that Balzac stages the appearance of the brilliant new novelist, Honoré de Balzac, and 'kills off' his younger, unsuccessful avatar, Horace de Saint-Aubin; *La Dernière Fée* marks a transitional phase between the Balzac known as 'Horace de Saint-Aubin' and Balzac the creator of *La Comédie humaine*). The protagonist,

Abel, rereads his book of fairy tales again and again, reinforcing his belief that the fairy stories within it are real, and thus cementing his 'certainty' that he will one day meet a fairy. The protagonist never finds out that his belief was misguided, for a 'fairy' does indeed appear, and thus Abel's illusions are not dispelled. (In reality, the 'fairy' is a wealthy duchess, who has heard of the beautiful and naïve Abel and of his preoccupation with fairies, and has decided to amuse herself by staging his fantasy.) As we have seen, echoes of this kind of fantasy are implicit in Balzac's letters to the *Étrangère*. In an allegorical, roundabout way, Balzac suggests in this early work how the kind of rereading we do in childhood — rereading a favourite book over and over, convinced of its seriousness — can become reflected in adult life, in the way adults cling to preconceptions and illusions (which rereading can reinforce) (*PR*, II, 38).

One novel in which the idea of rereading — letters, but also poetry and novels — is given a particular significance is *Modeste Mignon* (a novel which of course was not only based on the early Balzac-Hanska correspondence, but which was the result of a curious collaboration between the two: Hanska provided the initial idea, and Balzac took it up and wrote it).[62] In this novel, a mysterious 'O d'Este-M' (in reality, an unremarkable though precocious young woman named Modeste) is corresponding with someone she believes to be the famous poet, Canalis, unaware that it is in fact the poet's secretary (Ernest de la Brière) who is writing back, and with whom she is falling in love. Some carefully constructed narratives about their respective situations, as well as some covert gazing, leads them to believe that they are falling in love, despite not knowing anything about one another.[63]

Tellingly, the protagonists frequently refer to their correspondence as a 'novel', or a 'poem'.[64] The correspondents are treating their letter-writing as though it were a fiction, and using it to fuel their pre-conceived, idealized fantasies; in a way, this serves to bring their rereadings of one another's letters closer to the kind of naïve childhood reading undertaken by Abel. For instance, the heroine wants to find in her rereadings of poetry and letters only the poor, lonely poet of her dreams, whom she might be able to look after. This novel, which was directly inspired by the Balzac-Hanska correspondence, contains parallels between the way in which characters misuse rereading and the way in which Balzac himself rereads. Indeed, rereading appears to be a significant (if little-discussed) trope in *Modeste Mignon*.

The plot of this novel centres on an exchange of letters; it also hinges on several acts of deception. Firstly, the misleading image of the poet Canalis in a bookseller's window seduces the young Modeste (despite the bookseller's advice, and despite the mocking letter she then receives from Canalis's editor) into writing to him. Secondly, the insincere quality of the hypocritical, seductive poetry of Canalis reinforces her belief in all the illusions and fancies she had entertained about this author. Thirdly, the letter which she sends to Canalis is deliberately evasive and falsely modest; he and Ernest rightly divine in it a thinly veiled attempt to seduce the poet. Fourthly, the reply which Modeste receives, with the arms of Canalis embossed on the envelope, is in fact written by his secretary, Ernest, masquerading as Canalis. And finally, his reply prompts Modeste to lie to him, hinting that she has a large fortune.

Balzac takes care to describe in detail the characters' reactions upon receiving the first letter from their correspondent: Ernest musing over the anonymous letter of the unknown young woman, Modeste spending a sleepless night over Ernest's reply. Both characters read and reread the first letter they receive, searching, apparently in vain, for some hidden significance beyond the level of the words. Ernest, we are told, 'lut la lettre de Modeste, et la relut en essayant d'en deviner l'esprit caché' [read Modeste's letter and reread it, trying to work out its hidden message] (*CH*, I, 521). Modeste, too, reads and rereads the first communication she receives, and we are told that 'elle étudia cette prose étudiée' [she studied this studied prose] of Ernest's letter (*CH*, I , 525). This roundabout repetition of the verb 'étudier' reminds us that the letter she is rereading was a carefully crafted construct: there was nothing 'genuine' about Ernest's letter in the first place, and therefore rereading it, and attempting to find in it a deeper level of meaning, is a futile pursuit. (At certain points, the letter is almost parroting some of the things which came up in Ernest's earlier conversation with the cynical Canalis, during which Modeste's letter was discussed.) Is Balzac effectively showing us that the most sincere-sounding texts cannot wholly be trusted? Ernest's letter is a frank and candid account of how to avoid acts of self-deception and what we might call *mauvaise foi*; yet we know that this letter is shrouded in all sorts of hypocrisies and lies, ones which cannot be exposed by a careful rereading; to do this, the reader would have required access to additional information.

Through his portrayal of rereading in *Modeste Mignon*, Balzac is demonstrating its limitations. Rereading can indeed reveal inner depths, but only if the text being reread has a degree of sincerity and openness; otherwise the rereader comes up against the barrier of a text carefully constructed to be 'closed'. Hence, for example, there is little point in Modeste's study of Ernest's already studied prose. Balzac seems to be arguing that there is a limit to what we can glean from rereading a letter; if someone has carefully crafted it to conceal certain information, the text does not necessarily always have an opening, no matter how hard it is probed.

Both Modeste and Ernest come across such barriers in one another's letters; and both persist in studying the letters, attempting to tease out some interesting meaning, but effectively just judging the letter according to their own desires. For Ernest, who wishes desperately that a woman would attempt to seduce him in just such a way ('Oh! combien j'aimerais une femme venue à moi!' [Oh! How I would love a woman who had come to me!], *CH*, I, 521), rereading the first letter of Modeste only serves to reconfirm his initial curiosity — despite Canalis's attempt to tell him that the letter is likely to be misleading. In Ernest's case, Balzac appears to suggest that rereading will only serve to confirm what one already knows, or believes. For Modeste, who dreams of seducing a great poet, Ernest's candid and, to her mind, cruel reply, only spurs her on to try and win over the poet: 'Aussi [...] Modeste éprouva-t-elle en son cœur un effroyable désir de l'emporter sur cet esprit de rectitude et de le précipiter dans quelque contradiction, de lui rendre ce coup de massue' [Thus [...] Modeste felt a terrible desire in her heart to defeat this spirit of rectitude and to force him into some contradiction or other, to return the heavy blow] (*CH*, I, 525). In Modeste's case, then, while it revealed unwelcome truths, reading and rereading the letter only served to reconfirm her in her own beliefs and desires.

Ernest rereads a later letter by Modeste in order to gorge himself on the 'subtil poison' [subtle poison] of the compliments of a 'menteuse charmante' [charming liar] (*CH*, I, 589). Here, the act of rereading forms part of a ridiculous scene in which Ernest preens and admires himself in front of a mirror, turning this way and that, and rereading the flattering letter plays a part in this wilful self-deception. The same is true of Modeste's rereading of the poetry of Canalis in order to cheer herself up after the mocking letter from Canalis's editor falls flat on her fantasies, 'comme un pavé sur une tulipe' [like a paving stone on a tulip], destroying her fancy of the poet as a lonely dreamer, living in an attic (*CH*, I, 512). We are told that 'D'ailleurs, elle relut les poésies de Canalis, vers excessivement pipeurs, pleins d'hypocrisie' [Besides, she reread the poetry of Canalis, those excessively misleading verses, full of hypocrisy] (Ibid.). Modeste fails to spot this hypocrisy, and rereading the poems helps her to readopt her earlier convictions. 'Modeste, en reprenant ses impressions, eut confiance en cette âme, en cette physionomie [...]. Elle n'écouta pas le libraire' [In going back to her earlier impressions, Modeste placed her trust in this character, in this physiognomy [...]. She did not listen to the bookseller] (*CH*, I, 513). The warnings of both the bookseller and the editor (both of whom, by profession, are in a sense keepers of texts, more accustomed than Modeste to reading with a critical eye, and to determining the true 'value' of a piece of writing) go unheeded.

In this novel, then, in which the ultimate meaning of the text remains closed, and in which the act of rereading results only in whatever the rereader wants, Balzac shows that there are limits to rereading. The plot of *Modeste Mignon* supports Balzac's comment that 'La profondeur vient de l'intelligence du lecteur et non de la pensée exprimée. Un livre est moins un effet qu'une cause' [Profoundness comes from the intelligence of the reader and not from the thought being expressed. A book is less of an effect than it is a cause].[65] It is the reader of the text (a book, or a letter) who essentially has the power to construct its meaning — even though, for this to be a productive activity, we have to be able to assume a certain amount of good faith or sincerity on the part of the text's original author.

Balzac's second readings of Madame Hanska's letters illustrate the point that it is the reader who constructs the meaning of a text. There are instances in the letters to Madame Hanska where he uses rereading with the conscious goal of overriding earlier reactions, or ignoring an unwelcome reality; in the extract below, from July 1842, we see him rereading her letters selectively, or rereading only certain parts of her letters, after a disagreeable impression left by the first reading:

> Je me cramponne à la dernière page de votre lettre; je ne crois qu'à cela, je me cache à moi-même les autres pages où vous me rendez la liberté, la plus atroce chose que vous puissiez faire, et je m'efforce d'oublier pour ne voir que ce que vous me dites de bon, de tendre et de fidèlement affectueux. [...] Dites que vous entendez tout ce qu'il y a de fraîcheur et d'enfance et de grâce dans mon cœur, pour vous seule au monde? Écrivez-moi promptement que, quoi qu'il arrive, nous sommes toujours en 1833.[66]

> [I cling on to the last page of your letter; I believe in nothing else, I am hiding
> those pages from myself in which you give me my freedom, the most horrible
> thing you could do, and I force myself to forget so that I can only see the
> good, tender and faithfully affectionate things you tell me. [...] Say that you
> understand how much freshness, and childish happiness, and grace there is
> for you in my heart, and only for you? Write to me promptly that, whatever
> happens, we are still in 1833.]

In this extract, Balzac only holds on to selected passages of her letter, hiding
others which he tries to forget. On another occasion, rereading is used to override
the anger produced by Madame Hanska's letter. Moreover, Balzac shows that he
chooses the moment of the second reading for maximum soothing impact: 'A
demain, je relirai v[otre] lettre; en ce moment, je suis trop agité' [Til tomorrow, I
shall reread your letter; at the moment I am too agitated].[67] He returns to reread
her letter the same night, after having gone to see a friend, 'pour échapper à moi-
même' [to escape from myself]:

> J'ai relu votre lettre, et j'ai vu là dans ce qui m'a chagriné l'un de ces mouvements
> sauvages auxquels vous vous abandonnez, et qui est sans doute doublé d'une
> affection bien vive. [...] En relisant tout ce que vous avez écrit sur vos jeunes
> années et sur l'année 33, [...] je me suis senti bien digne de tant de sentiments si
> nobles, si purs, si naïfs.[68]

> [I have reread your letter, and I could see that in those parts which upset me
> there was one of those unchecked movements to which you abandon yourself,
> and which no doubt is lined with a very strong affection. [...] Rereading
> everything you have told me about your younger years and the year 1833, [...] I
> felt well worthy of so many feelings of such nobility, purity, and naivety.]

Thus the second reading is shown to have softened his initial negative reaction to her
words. Whether this may be because her letter was essentially filled with affection
and Balzac's first reading was misguided, we can never know; however, what is of
real interest here is the way in which Balzac himself appears aware of the potential
of that second reading to alter his initial perception, and that he consciously plans
for the second reading to take place at a time when he will not be 'agitated', such
that it can be savoured to best effect. By this stage in the correspondence, he had
long acknowledged the 'fatal power' which the letter holds over its reader if it is read
at a bad moment, or if it brings unwelcome news; he had previously expressed to
Madame Hanska the wish that there could be developed a system of signs between
two lovers, so that the moment of the first reading could be more appropriately
chosen:

> Les lettres sont douées d'une fatale puissance, elles possèdent une force qui se
> trouve en raison des sensations au milieu desquelles elles nous surprennent. Je
> voudrais qu'entre deux amis bien sûrs d'eux-mêmes, il y eût des signes convenus
> pour qu'à l'aspect d'une lettre chacun d'eux sût si la lettre est d'une expansive
> gaieté ou d'un gémissement plaintif, on aurait le choix du moment pour la
> lire.[69]

> [Letters are invested with a fatal power, they possess a force which owes much
> to the feelings amid which they happen upon us. I wish that between two

friends who are sure of themselves there could be some agreed signs, so that at
the sight of a letter each of them knows if the letter is of an expansive gaiety or
if it is a plaintive whine. One might then choose the right moment to read it.]

This sense of vulnerability at the first reading can be overcome, as we see in the
above examples, through a carefully directed rereading.

   In the following quotation from his *Correspondance,* Balzac makes an explicit
link between rereading and literary creation, or storytelling; he needs to reread
in order to write. '*Louis Lambert* m'a coûté tant de travaux! que d'ouvrages il m'a
fallu relire pour écrire ce livre!' [*Louis Lambert* cost me so much effort! How many
works have I had to reread to write this book!] (*Corr*, II, 89). In Balzac's letter-
exchange with Madame Hanska, rereading and the production of text likewise
appear inextricably linked. There is an instance in Balzac's letters to her where, in
the absence of further communication from the mistress, her last letter is read and
reread, and incites Balzac to write multiple replies. The 'lettre cachetée en noir'
[black-sealed letter][70] — equivalent to the 'black-bordered letters' in which deaths
were announced in Victorian England — refers to the letter from Madame Hanska
to Balzac, received in January 1842 (exact date unknown), in which she announces
her husband's death.

   Monsieur Hanski's death led Madame Hanska to reflect upon her relationship
with Balzac, and eventually to try and break it off, setting them both free. She had
a daughter to think of; also, alone and free for the first time since she was married
at the age of fourteen, perhaps she did not find the idea of tying herself down to a
man again appealing. Balzac describes reading and rereading the letter of rejection:
'votre lettre que je viens de relire encore, comme pour y chercher des raisons contre
le chagrin qu'elle m'a causé, qui m'a tenu tout éveillé pendant cette nuit' [your
letter, which I have just reread again, as though to search in it for reasons not to
succumb to the grief it has caused me, which has kept me awake all night].[71]

   Between Balzac receiving the black-sealed letter, and the arrival of her subsequent
letter (with its impending rejection), there is a silence of over six weeks on Madame
Hanska's side. Balzac's hopeful request, on 5 January 1842, for her to promise him
her hand receives no reply until 21 February 1842. During her silence, for want
of any further letters, he rereads the black-sealed letter over and over again, and
writes several different replies.[72] Madame Hanska's letter appears, in a sense, to be
a 'closed' text; effectively, the silent Éveline has 'disabled' Balzac in his role as her
correspondent, requiring no reply, no action from him. Balzac describes how he
sought in it 'deux mots pour moi' [two words for me], which he did not find.[73] The
letter apparently gives no concrete answers, but instead leaves Balzac with many
questions.

   Balzac writes six letters to Madame Hanska (dated 5, 10, 20, 22, and 31 January,
and 1 February) before finally receiving her reply. Thus, in the absence of any
further communication from her, he generates a large amount of text, much of
which seems to be prompted by rereadings of her last letter (on three occasions, he
alludes specifically to having reread it).[74]

   In his letter of 10 January 1842, Balzac describes his second reading of the letter
announcing the husband's death:

> Vous allez savoir que je relis toujours plusieurs fois vos lettres, or en relisant, j'ai été saisi d'un froid mortel en faisant peser mon âme sur les vingt dernières lignes où vous me dites vous si mal porter que vous m'exprimez des craintes funestes.[75]

> [And you shall know that I always reread your letters; well, as I was rereading it, I was seized by a mortal chill when focusing on the final twenty lines in which you tell me that you are so unwell that you are expressing your macabre fears.]

If the initial reading resulted in a calm reaction and even some pleasure (and also uncertainty), the second, according to Balzac, in which he fixated on the unsettling last lines of the letter, caused pure terror:

> Non, rien ne peut vous exprimer quel coup profond m'a atteint en lisant dans le journal ces lignes: *La Gazette de* Posen *nous apprend la mort de la comtesse Kicka* [...]. Il est si facile d'imprimer un K pour un H [...] que je n'ai pu retenir un cri, [...] l'on m'a porté dans mon lit où j'ai eu depuis deux jours une fièvre nerveuse qui vient de se calmer, et me voici, relisant encore votre lettre, et vous écrivant.[76]

> [No, nothing can tell you what a deep shock I had when I read the following lines in a newspaper: *The* Posen *Gazette tells us of the death of the countess Kicka* [...]. It is so easy to print a K for an H [...] that I could not hold back a cry, [...] they carried me to my bed where for the last two days I have had a nervous fever which has only just subsided, and here I am, rereading your letter again, and writing to you.]

He writes to her again on 20 and 22 January; these two letters describe his unexpected new habit of sleeping fourteen hours a day (p. 553) and confidently picturing himself with her; Balzac writes that he is certain of his impending union with Madame Hanska. In the letter of 22 January, he expresses his impatience to hear from her and to know more than what her letter has conveyed.

When he sits down to write to her again, on 31 January 1842, Balzac again alludes to rereading her letter, and describes a completely different reaction to his earlier readings: his response is now that of a concerned family friend, offering sensible financial advice:

> J'ai relu encore votre lettre, et crois que j'ai encore bien des choses à vous en dire. Et d'abord, vous devez reconnaître que j'avais bien raison dans des conseils que je vous donnais à Genève relativement à la gestion de votre fortune. [...] Voulez-vous me permettre, à moi votre ami [...], de vous donner un conseil?[77]

> [I have reread your letter again, and I think I still have many things to tell you. And first of all, you must see that I was right in all the advice I gave you in Geneva, relating to the management of your fortune. [...] Would you permit me, as your friend [...], to give you some advice?]

Each rereading, then, results in a completely different reaction; we could argue that each rereading is, in a sense, a 'de-reading', insofar as it tries to do away with the perceptions created by earlier readings.[78] As Balzac approaches the text of Madame Hanska's letter, he tries to gauge the most appropriate response to make, and the role he ought to play — should he respond as the happy suitor, the anguished lover, or the indispensable counsellor and friend? In the face of her sphinx-like silence,

Balzac is like a medium attempting a 'cold reading', firing out reply after reply, and trying to gauge which response will get a positive reaction.

What we are seeing here is that rereading can be an act of desperation; the text is reread when its meaning has remained inaccessible and there is nothing else to go on. Balzac has read and reread the letter and he finds himself stumped. Rereading is therefore not necessarily an act which results in increased knowledge, or in an expansion of our understanding; there is, in fact, something tragic about Balzac's endless rereadings of some of Hanska's letters. His multiple rereadings of the early letter from her in which she depicts her ideas at the age of twenty-seven are reminiscent of Abel's rereadings of his fairy tales, clinging to his first impressions of the story and hoping a fairy will come.[79]

Likewise in the case of the 'black-sealed letter' we see Balzac engaged in an act of selective rereading which, overriding a previous reading and other conclusions that might be drawn from the context, allows Balzac to reach or cling to a more hopeful possibility. In fact, the last two letters in the collection before the 'black-sealed letter' (both dating back to September 1841) already contained strong hints of an impending rejection.[80] In view of this earlier evidence that the relationship was already in difficulties, we might view Balzac's optimistic rereadings of Madame Hanska's announcement of her husband's death as somewhat misguided. However, the fact that the relationship continued and flourished, in spite of all the obstacles in its path, suggests that Balzac's hunch to carry on 'de-reading' Éveline's letters was correct, and that his relentless drive to produce new narratives succeeded in breathing new life into the relationship.

The pattern that emerges from all this is that Balzac tells them both certain stories about their epistolary relationship, trying to reinforce his belief in its sustainability, and in the possibility of its desired conclusion (a life spent together). When he tries to prompt her to write to him in a certain way ('Tell me', 'Write to me'), he is asking her permission to allow him to continue writing, undisrupted, this most significant correspondence of his life. When this is not forthcoming, Balzac turns to a selective rereading of those letters of hers which tell him what he wishes to hear, or takes refuge in daydreams and memories of the past:

> Je dévalle dans le rêve, dans le plaisir de revenir dans le passé; je vis en pensant à v[ous] et aux deux enfants. Toute la puissance de mon imagination est au service de mes souvenirs. Je regrimpe le Simplon et je ris à v[otre] perfide prière d'aller voir les Monigault pour avoir le droit de me les jeter à la tête. Je me retrouve à la soirée de di Negro dans le magnifique salon Féder, et la magnifique chambre à coucher. Ou en Hollande, grondé sur le quai de Rotterdam, et quelles paroles! Vous vous opposiez systématiquement à tout ce que je voulais faire. [...] Et l'affaire de Tourtemagne où j'ai failli retourner me jeter dans la cascade, tant vous m'aviez abattu. Enfin, je relis la lettre où vous m'avez dépeint vos sublimes idées de 27 ans, lorsque vous êtes partie pour aller à Neufchâtel.[81]

> [I hurtle down into my daydreams, into the pleasure of retracing the past; I keep alive by thinking of you and the two children. All the power of my imagination is being deployed in the service of my memories. I climb the Simplon again, I laugh at your devious request to go and see the Monigaults just for the pleasure of teasing me. I find myself once again at di Negro's party in the magnificent

Féder salon, and the magnificent bedchamber. Or in Holland, being scolded on the Rotterdam quay, and what words! You were systematically opposing yourself to everything I wanted to do. [...] And the Tourtemagne affair, where I very nearly turned and threw myself under the waterfall, you had so discouraged me. Finally, I reread the letter where you depicted your sublime ideas at the age of 27, when you had just left for Neufchâtel.]

Once again, the important point here is that what counts for Balzac is the opportunity to continue writing. Balzac can bear Madame Hanska's silence, up to a point; he is able to employ rereading as a mechanism to help him deal with this and go on producing texts of his own. More disturbing to him is the idea that, should her silence continue indefinitely, his own textual production directed at her would have to cease, and this conclusion, as we have seen, is one that he will go to considerable lengths to avoid.

We have seen that Balzac's passion for collecting is intimately bound up with the relationship with Éveline Hanska; his correspondence with her serves both as a record and an extension of his personal collection. Furthermore, we have seen that, for Balzac, collecting is bound up with the act of rereading; preserving and collecting the letters allows them to be re-interrogated and re-enjoyed, and thereby to serve as source material for Balzac's own writings. As we saw in the case of *Louis Lambert,* Balzac found it necessary to reread numerous works in order for the ideas behind that novel to take shape (*Corr,* II, 89). This process is echoed in the creation of Balzac's own letters to Madame Hanska, the rereading of her letters functioning as source material for the numerous narrative fancies that are developed in the letters.

We therefore should not think of Balzac's storytelling as somehow separate from other aspects of his life such as the relationship with Madame Hanska or his penchant for collecting objects. Rather, these elements interweave with Balzac's storytelling practice, facilitate it, and furnish it with material and opportunities for development. From 1833 onwards the Hanska correspondence becomes not just an additional element but a fundamental thread running through Balzac's life, one that serves to bind together many other aspects of his being, such as collecting, reading and rereading, and the development of narratives. This analysis has demonstrated that there existed in Balzac's storytelling a kind of cycle between the acts of writing, receiving and hoarding letters, rereading them, and then using them in the genesis of further writings.

'La relecture [...] n'est tolérée que chez certaines catégories marginales de lecteurs (les enfants, les vieillards et les professeurs)' [Rereading [...] is tolerated only in certain marginal categories of readers (children, old people, and professors)].[82] As Roland Barthes points out in *S/Z,* rereading is an activity very frequently engaged in by children. The familiarity of an already-known story is a source of reassurance and pleasure to children (repetition in itself is often a source of childhood pleasure). For adults, rereading can more frequently be a nostalgic activity, not only a source of familiar pleasures but also a method of recalling a happier time, or an earlier, happier self. In Balzac's case, we have seen this clearly in his rereadings of Madame Hanska's early letters (which he said made him feel as if he were still in 1833). We have also seen a trace of this process in his use of names or nicknames for his adult female correspondents that evoke childhood or motherhood to him (as discussed in Chapter 1). Balzac appears to have used new relationships with adult women as a way of repeating, or perhaps we might say, returning to (or re-understanding) his childhood relationship with his mother.

The example of the blank page shows how the act of rereading can spark creation and storytelling. It can only have been on Balzac's detailed (re-)consideration of Hanska's letters that the blank page acquired significance for him. Insofar as it even occurred to him to use the idea of the blank page as an important symbol, he is likely to have been poring over every detail of her letters — including details that were only present as absences. The fact that Balzac focuses so much on such details indicates the depth to which he was rereading these letters, using the act of rereading as a springboard for his creation.

Furthermore, we have seen how the action of continually rereading and re-interpreting letters allows for the kind of reinvention of the correspondence and the self which we saw earlier in this chapter. When we saw Balzac rereading the letter announcing Monsieur Hanski's death, and trying various 'voices' with which to reply — the confident fiancé, the swooning Romantic lover, the concerned friend — we witnessed how the possibility of rereading allowed Balzac to attempt to choose the most appropriate role.

Rereading therefore emerges as a way of taking possession, gaining control, assimilating, understanding, sifting, and internalizing the contents, so that these may then enter the storyteller's store of concepts and images, which can then be integrated into new creative actions. Balzac's rereadings of the letters might thus be regarded as analogous to putting concepts into storage, like the objects Balzac collects. They can then be taken out again by Balzac as required, and used in future creations.

Balzac's continual writing, both of letters and of novels, betrays a need to exert some form of control over the external world. In 1843 he wrote to Madame Hanska:

> Il me faut le travail et les créations littéraires pour que je sois maître de moi, vous ne sauriez [croire] à quel point je deviens stupide dès que je suis livré à moi-même [...]. Si je ne me mets pas au lit, fatigué de travaux et succombant au sommeil, je suis perdu; car le moment où, avant le sommeil, on se retrouve face à face avec soi-même et les champs immenses du possible, ce moment est fatal pour moi.[83]

> [I need my work and my literary creations in order for me to be master of my own self; you would not believe how stupid I become as soon as I am left to my own devices [...]. If I do not go to bed tired out by work and yielding easily to sleep, I am lost; for that moment where, just before falling asleep, one comes face to face with oneself, and with the immense field of possibilities, that moment is fatal to me.]

This extract, from a letter in which Balzac conveys his longing for the absent Hanska, can be read as a more general comment (as the change to the more impersonal pronoun 'on' suggests) on his attempts to limit the danger of being overwhelmed by the power of the external world. To liberate their creative potential, such people need to find mechanisms to tie down their anxiety and reassure themselves that the outside world is at least to some degree under control, that it no longer contains elements which remain menacingly outside the narratives that they use to explain the world to themselves. For Balzac, rereading and the re-examination of collected objects, and the continual shaping of new narratives to explain them in more and more emotionally satisfying ways, was one such technique.

Notes to Chapter 3

1. Balzac uses the word 'bricabracomanie' in *Le Cousin Pons* (*CH*, VII, 764). In the *Lettres à Madame Hanska*, there are many references to the activity of 'bric-a-bracking' ('bricabracquer'); for example *LMH*, II, 239 (1 July 1846), *LMH*, II, 593 (23 June 1847), *LMH*, II, 826 (5 May 1848), and *LMH*, I, 921 (21 October 1844).
2. *LMH*, I, 921 (21 October 1844).
3. See *Corr*, I, 11.
4. On the representation of objects in *La Comédie humaine*, see Juliette Frølich, 'Balzac, l'objet et les archives romantiques de la création', *L'Année balzacienne* (2000), 145–57, and *Des hommes, des femmes et des choses: langages de l'objet de Balzac à Proust* (Saint-Denis: Presses Universitaires de Vincennes, 1997), p. 17.
5. Emma Bielecki, *The Collector in Nineteenth-Century Literature: Representation, Identity, Knowledge* (Bern: Peter Lang, 2012), p. 45. See also Janell Watson, *Literature and Material Culture from Balzac to Proust* (Cambridge: Cambridge University Press, 1999).
6. See Hunt, p. 390.
7. See also Adrien Goetz, '"De si vives compensations à la faillite de la gloire": les collectionneurs au centre de *La Comédie humaine*', in *Balzac et la peinture* (Tours: Musée des Beaux-Arts de Tours/ Farrago, 1999), pp. 187–92 (p. 188).
8. See Goetz, p. 189, and Bielecki, pp. 81 & 83.
9. Tim Farrant, *Balzac's Shorter Fictions: Genesis and Genre* (Oxford: Oxford University Press, 2002), p. 268.
10. Cited in Bielecki, p. 49.
11. 'Ces choses si grandes et si petites, si magnifiques et si *rien*! qui font d'une paille tout un musée pour le cœur!' [These things so great and so small, so magnificent and so like *nothing*! And which can turn a mere straw into a whole museum for the heart!] (*LMH*, I, p. 80, 29 October 1833). The context here suggests that it is the act of giving a gift which bestows upon the object itself special significance.
12. *LMH*, I, 84 (3 November 1833). See also *LMH*, I, 78 (29 October 1833); *LMH*, I, 102 (1 December 1833), where Balzac describes kissing flower petals; and *LMH*, I, 178 (30 July 1834), where he speaks of holding a flower between his lips while writing.
13. *LMH*, I, 54 (9 September 1833).
14. *LMH*, I, 142 (22 February 1834).
15. Bielecki describes the fetishist as 'the collector's decadent brother' (p. 92).
16. *LMH*, II, 28 (26 February 1845).
17. Goetz, p. 189.
18. *LMH*, I, 798 (2 February 1844).
19. *LMH*, I, 928 (8 November 1844).
20. See Goetz, p. 187. On the subject of the collections contained in the rue Fortunée house, see Jarry.
21. *LMH*, II, 544 (27 February 1847).
22. *LMH*, II, 560 (30 May 1847). See also *LMH*, II, 559, 562, & 577, for other references to the *écrin*. Years later, Freud would famously associate a 'jewel-case' with female genitalia in the 'Dora' case history.
23. *LMH*, I, 839 (7 April 1844).
24. *LMH*, II, 529 (20 January 1847).
25. Ibid.
26. See *LMH*, II, 905.

27. *LMH*, II, 592 (22 June 1847).

28. *LMH*, I, 598 (8 August 1842).

29. *LMH*, II, 681 (3 September 1847).

30. Baron, *Hiéroglyphes*, p. 95.

31. *LMH*, I, 148 (11 March 1834).

32. The full quotation reads: 'Votre lettre triste que je relis, car c'est notre seule volupté, c'est de n[ous] lire et de n[ous] relire' [Your sad letter which I reread, for that is our only delight, to read and reread one another] (*LMH*, II, 972, 17 August 1848). The French word *volupté* also has a sensual, or sexual, connotation.

33. *LMH*, I, 174 (15 July 1834).

34. See for example *LMH*, I, 26 (January 1833), *LMH*, I, 112 (January 1834), *LMH*, I, 141 (21 February 1834), and, in later years, *LMH*, II, 503 (1 January 1847).

35. *LMH*, I, 419 (7 November 1837). The extract continues with a reference to Swedenborg.

36. See for example *LMH*, I, 175–76. The literal translation is 'a fly's footprints'.

37. Perfume, in Balzac's esoteric writings, is a pure and immediate form of communication. See *Louis Lambert*, where 'Les parfums sont des idées peut-être' [Perfumes are ideas perhaps] (*CH*, XI, 396); *Séraphîta*, where perfume engenders thought (*CH*, XI, 483); and *Massimila Doni*, where the communicative immediacy of perfume is comparable only to that of music (*CH*, X 350).

38. *LMH*, I, 634 (20 January 1843).

39. See *LMH*, I, 419 (7 November 1837).

40. *LMH*, II, 119 (12 December 1845), my emphasis.

41. See *LMH*, II, 119–21 & 140–41. The editors of the correspondence also note a similar post-script in Balzac's letter of 13 November 1845, *LMH, II*, 98–100.

42. *LMH*, II, 119 (12 December 1845).

43. Ibid.

44. *LMH*, II, 120 (12 December 1845).

45. Manuscript A. 302, fol. 378, cited in *LMH*, II, 121, n. 1. Note that in this extract he lists twenty-four cities, whereas in the above-cited extract from the letter of 12 December 1845 he referred to twenty-three.

46. *LMH*, I, 798 (2 February 1844).

47. *LMH*, II, 155 (7 January 1846).

48. Patricia Meyer Spacks, *On Rereading* (Cambridge, MA, & London: Belknap, 2011), p. 2.

49. *LMH*, I, 25 (January 1833).

50. *LMH*, II, 905 (30 August 1844).

51. *LMH*, II, 158 (10 January 1846).

52. *LMH*, I, 203 (26 October 1834).

53. Vladimir Nabokov, *Lectures on Literature*, (London: Harvest, 1980) p. 3. Roland Barthes also suggests that there is no such thing as a first reading, in 'Écrire la lecture', in *Le Bruissement de la langue* (Paris: Seuil, 1984), pp. 22–23. On reading and rereading as a single concept, see also Calinescu, *Rereading*, pp. xi-xii.

54. To compare the number of references to rereading in his various correspondence, see the 'Concordance' by Kazuo Kiriu, <http://www.v2asp.paris.fr/commun/v2asp/musees/balzac/kiriu/> [accessed 8 February 2013].

55. See 'Préface de la première édition', *CH*, II, 261–72 (especially pp. 264–66).

56. Balzac admits that to 'certains gens logiques' [certain logical people] this system may seem a 'vice capital' [capital vice] but hopes that 'Peut-être ce vice passera-t-il plus tard pour une beauté' [Perhaps this vice may later pass for beauty] (p. 264) — a modest hope for what was subsequently to become his most famous literary device.

57. For inconsistencies in Balzac's process of creating recurring characters, see Fernand Lotte, 'Le Retour des personnages dans *La Comédie humaine*: avantages et inconvénients du procédé,' *L'Année balzacienne* (1961), 227–81.

58. See Jeannine Guichardet, 'Penser/voir avec Balzac: le Paris d'hier et d'aujourd'hui', in *Penser avec Balzac*, ed. by José-Luis Diaz and Isabelle Tournier (Saint-Cyr-sur-Loire: Christian-Pirot, 2003), pp. 93–94.

59. See Antony R. Pugh, *Balzac's Recurring Characters* (London: Duckworth, 1975), p. 222. '[Balzac

is] implying that it is the second reading which really counts in his eyes, and that he expects his device of recurring characters to spur his readers on to explore more. Once again, he thinks his work will be more life-like as a result, and therefore more interesting, more intriguing'.

60. Marcel Proust, *Contre Sainte-Beuve*, ed. by Pierre Clarac and Yves Sandre (Paris: Gallimard, 1954), p. 213.
61. See, for example, some of the references to re-reading letters in *Mémoires de deux jeunes mariées*: *CH*, I, 303, 313, 323, 326, 372, & 384. A meticulous letter-writer like Renée de Maucombe might reread her correspondent's letter carefully before penning her full reply; multiple readings can bring clarity, or reveal strong feelings. 'Je viens de la relire [ta lettre], et suis effrayée des vulgarités de sentiment qu'elle contient' [I have just reread [your letter], and I am shocked by the vulgarity of sentiment which it contains] (*CH*, I, 323); 'en te relisant une invincible et profonde terreur m'a saisie' [rereading your words, a deep and unshakeable terror came over me] (*CH*, I, 313). Rereading also brings insights: 'je relisais tes lettres et j'y découvrais je ne sais quelle mélancolie cachée' [I was rereading your letters and discovering in them a mysterious hidden melancholy] (*CH*, I, 303).
62. For details of the genesis of *Modeste Mignon*, see Maurice Regard, 'Introduction', *CH*, I, 447–67.
63. I discuss the significance of 'gazing unseen' in this novel in my article 'An Aesthetics of Indirection in Novels and Letters', p. 243.
64. See Schuerewegen, *Balzac contre Balzac*, pp. 111–12.
65. Balzac, *Pensées, sujets, fragments*, p. 9.
66. *LMH*, I, 587 (12 July 1842).
67. *LMH*, II, 612 (2 July 1847).
68. *LMH*, II, 612–13 (2 July 1847).
69. *LMH*, I, 335 (1 October 1836). See also *LMH*, II, 613 (2 July 1847, evening).
70. *LMH*, I, 545 (5 January 1842).
71. *LMH*, I, 559 (22 February 1842).
72. *LMH*, I, 554 (31 January 1842); *LMH*, I, 554 (22 January 1842); and *LMH*, I, 556 (21 February 1842), when he receives the devastating reply.
73. *LMH*, I, 546 (5 January 1842).
74. See letters dated 10 and 31 January.
75. *LMH*, I, 549 (10 January 1842).
76. Ibid.
77. *LMH*, I, 554 (31 January 1842).
78. I borrow the concept of 'de-reading' from Tim Farrant. See Farrant, 'Burying the Past: De-reading *Dominique*', in *Re-Reading/La Relecture: Essays in Honour of Graham Falconer*, ed. by Rachel Falconer and Andrew Oliver (Newcastle upon Tyne: Cambridge Scholars, 2012), pp. 49–66. On 'de-reading', see especially pp. 53 & 61.
79. *LMH*, II, 636 (22 July 1847).
80. See for instance *LMH*, I, 538 (September 1841), in which Balzac complains of 'le chagrin que m'a causé votre silence' [the sorrow that your silence caused me], and 539–42 (30 September 1841), where it is clear that Hanska's reply to this complaint was not favourable.
81. *LMH*, II, 636 (22 July 1847).
82. Roland Barthes, *S/Z* (Paris: Seuil, 1970), p. 22.
83. *LMH*, I, 633 (17 January 1843).

AFTERWORD

❖

The Afterlife of the Letters

Il prit froidement les lettres et les jeta dans le foyer [...].

Des fragments roulèrent sur les cendres en lui laissant voir des commencements de phrase, des mots, des pensées à demi-brûlées, et qu'il se plut à saisir dans la flamme par un divertissement machinal.

'Assise à ta porte attendu... Caprice j'obéis... Des rivales... moi, non! ta Pauline... aime plus de Pauline donc? [...] Amour éternel... Mourir...

[Indifferently, he took the letters and threw them into the fireplace [...].

Fragments fell onto the embers, letting him glimpse the start of a sentence here, a word there, elsewhere a half-burned thought; he amused himself by spotting these amongst the flames, with a kind of mechanical enjoyment.

'Sitting at your door waiting... Whim, I obey... Rivals... me, never! Your Pauline... no longer love Pauline? [...] Eternal love... To die...]

BALZAC, *La Peau de chagrin* (*CH*, x, 287)

The story of Balzac and his Eve ends, as many love stories do, with a wedding. The letters, which retrospectively resemble one long marriage plot, come to an end in September 1848, just before Balzac travelled to what is now the Ukraine to join Madame Hanska. He married her on 14 March 1850. The epistolary relationship which began with anonymous letters and newspaper announcements thus ends, as fairy-tale relationships might, with a marriage and a promise of 'happily ever after'.

Already suffering from ill health since the beginning of 1850, Balzac arrived back in Paris on 20 or 21 May, after a lengthy and difficult four-week journey, in very bad shape. Upon arrival in the rue Fortunée, the pair found that the door to their house was locked. When a locksmith forced it open, they discovered that the servant who had been looking after the house had gone insane; a strange and ominous start to their life together.

Balzac's health continued to deteriorate steadily. He took to his bed shortly after his return, and never recovered. A consultation with several doctors on 30 May resulted in one of the doctors telling Victor Hugo that Balzac had only six weeks to live.[1] Éveline became his secretary as well as his nurse, taking down dictation for any letters he needed to write. The last known writing in Balzac's hand is on the bottom of a letter written by Éveline on 20 June to Théophile Gautier; the shaky scrawl says 'Je ne puis plus lire ni écrire' [I can no longer read or write].[2] Victor Hugo described visiting an unconscious Balzac on the night of his death in his memoir *Choses vues* [Things Seen]. Balzac died on 18 August 1850, never having enjoyed the paradise he had built for his Eve.

It was perhaps in writing the letters themselves that Balzac came closest to finding his 'paradise' — as this extract from his letters to Madame Hanska suggests: 'Vous écrire, c'est tomber dans le paradis de mes souvenirs et dans l'enfer des espérances retardées, et [...] alors, je m'absorbe, je rêve; vous, c'est ma débauche, c'est mes rêveries heureuses, c'est les flâneries de mon âme!' [To write to you is to fall into the paradise of my memories and into the hell of my postponed hopes, and [...] then I lose myself in daydreams; you are my debauchery, my happy reverie, the meanderings of my soul!][3] Like his fictional avatar Félix de Vandenesse, as a child, the neglected Balzac very likely did a great deal of day-dreaming. Anne-Marie Baron has already pointed out that he describes creative inspiration in similar terms to Freud: as a 'rêve éveillé' [waking dream].[4] Throughout his life, Balzac retained these very positive associations with daydreaming, which seems to have been among the happier moments of his childhood; therefore, it is unsurprising that he links his enjoyment of the correspondence with Madame Hanska back to childhood daydreams. Already in his first surviving letter to her, we have seen him allude to the 'rêves' [dreams] and 'rêveries' [reveries] which accompany and fuel the letter-writing process.[5] Writing to Éveline in the above extract from April 1842, Balzac returns to this link between letter-writing and daydreaming, comparing the act of writing to her to a kind of happy reverie (whilst appearing to recognize, at the same time, that paradise cannot exist without a parallel hell).

By the time Balzac reached maturity, and his *Comédie humaine* was underway, storytelling had become his work, and therefore to an extent lost the positive associations with daydreaming that it had for him in his youth. Instead, those positive associations were now effectively transferred to the letter-writing, which retained a playfulness and dreaminess that Balzac could perhaps no longer employ as he wished in writing *La Comédie humaine*. 'Ordinairement, quand je puis vous écrire quelques lignes, c'est et ce fut toujours, le matin en me levant, en attendant que mes esprits reviennent et soient en état de reprendre les travaux de la veille' [Normally, whenever I have been able to write to you, it is and it always has been in the morning, when I get up, and while I am waiting for my faculties to return to me, and to be in a fit state to take up the previous night's work], Balzac wrote to Madame Hanska in the letter of April 1842. 'Vous êtes ainsi la continuation de mon sommeil, de mon temps heureux!' [You are thus the continuation of my sleep, of my happy time!][6]

Unlike his novels, these letters were not edited or published by Balzac and thus were not subject to his obsessive control (although, as we shall see, he did continue to exert a degree of posthumous influence). While their value lies in the insight they provide into the workings of Balzac's creative imagination, their survival, as we shall see, is only due to the efforts and indeed creative imaginations of others.

The history of the Balzac-Hanska letters does not stop with Balzac's death; rather, another story emerges, in which Madame Hanska reinvents herself (much like a Balzacian 'recurring character') as 'Ève de Balzac', editor and letter-writer in her own right. I have not concentrated in any detail on the character of Madame Hanska or on her side of the correspondence, showing only how she features in Balzac's imagination. Further research could focus in greater detail on her as a letter-writer, centering, for instance, on her letters to her daughter, her personal journal, and in particular on her letters to Champfleury and the echoes of her relationship to Balzac found therein.[7] Balzac's widow developed a friendship with the then thirty-year-old Champfleury, author of *Les Chats*, and this friendship grew into a brief love affair. In this correspondence she comes into her own, emerging as an elegant writer and astute critic, strong-minded and uncompromising. In one letter, she describes an evening spent with Balzac's relatives (whom she had come to detest) and in the company of her own sister, who was so bored that she kept asking in Polish if she could leave; Hanska appears to take a perverse pleasure in the incomprehension of Balzac's family.[8] Elsewhere, her letters also show some light-heartedness and a sense of humour; her younger lover Champfleury is affectionately referred to as 'Petiot' (which is the name of the fictitious rabbit in his own story *Chien-Caillou;* in English, the name means 'little one'). Without actually saying so, she is perhaps also staking a claim to being the literary giant of the two, while he, the published writer, is seen as a younger apprentice. She refers to him as:

> Mon pauvre petit lapin blond; car, après avoir bien réfléchi sur la nature de nos relations respectives, j'ai découvert qu'il y avait beaucoup en moi pour vous du sentiment de Chien-Caillou pour Petiot. C'est flatteur pour vous! Mais si Petiot continue à trouver spirituel le filandreux Mr. Cuvillier, il n'aura ni pain ni carottes.[9]

> [My poor little blonde rabbit; for, having thought about the nature of our relationship, I discovered that a lot of my feelings for you are like those of Chien-Caillou for Petiot. You should feel flattered! But if Petiot insists on finding the odious Mr Cuvillier 'witty', he will get neither carrots nor bread.]

Frequently, though she rejoices in her freedom and in her lack of accountability to anyone in particular, the letters also speak of loneliness and ill-health, throwing into relief her past pain:

> Je suis triste, mon Petiot, je suis malade, je suis accablée d'âme et de corps. — Enfin, que te dirais-je?... J'ai souffert ces deux derniers jours, comme je n'ai jamais souffert, moi, qui croyais avoir épuisé toutes les atroces variétés de la douleur.[10]

> [I am sad, my Petiot, I am ill, I am stricken down in body and soul. — Well, what can I say?... I have suffered these past two days as I have never suffered; I, who had believed myself to have exhausted all the possible atrocious kinds of pain.]

As we know, Balzac destroyed the bulk of Madame Hanska's letters to him at her request, in September 1847, afterwards periodically destroying her side of the correspondence. The three letters of hers to Balzac which remain paint only a very elusive picture of her own creative imagination.[11] The letters to Champfleury, along with those to her daughter and her personal journal, might go some way towards filling the gap left by those missing letters. (Several times, she instructed Champfleury to burn her letters; unlike Balzac, he did not comply.)[12]

Yet even in the correspondence with Balzac, from which she has effectively been effaced, Madame Hanska did not simply become reduced to the 'rôle ingrat de prête-nom' [thankless role of just a name on a page], which, as Martine Reid notes, is often the literary destiny of the correspondents of famous writers.[13] In the first instance, following Balzac's death, the former Hanska, now de Balzac, emerged as editor of Balzac's letters, some of which she consented to publish in 1876, but only after putting them through some considerable embroidering.[14] In her 1929 article, Irene Cornwell lists the kinds of changes which Hanska made (ranging from corrections of punctuation to actual added passages or omissions), and even points out one instance where the mistress-turned-editor adds a somewhat redundant 'fulsome paragraph' of her own, apparently attempting (unnecessarily) to clarify or enhance Balzac's prose with some patriotic-sounding musings that 'seem hardly good enough to warrant insertion in the body of the text'.[15]

Roger Pierrot draws the reader's attention to one curious example of the sorts of corrections undertaken by Ève de Balzac.[16] In the letter in question, Balzac told her how he would like her to be 'concise dans l'éloge, très prolixe dans la critique' [concise in [her] praise, very wordy in [her] criticism] when giving him her comments on his works, and he also praises her 'génie critique' [critical genius] in relation to comments she had recently made about one of his plays.[17] Balzac complimented her intelligent critique by telling her 'Oui, Planche n'aurait pas été plus savant' [Yes, Planche would not have been more knowledgeable].[18] In her edition of the letter, Éveline modifies and extends this sentence, inserting a supplementary clause: 'Oui, — ne vous défendez pas, ne faites pas votre petit geste familier, ne couvrez pas vos yeux de vos petites mains rondes et blanches — nos plus renommés critiques contemporains n'auraient pas été plus savants' [Yes — *do not defend yourself, do not make that familiar little gesture of yours; do not cover up your eyes with your little white and rounded hands* — our most renowned critics would not have been more knowledgeable).[19]

As Jean Pommier suggests in his analysis of this extract, Éveline's addition to the text, in which she attempts to show her modesty — the 'petit geste', which appears to cover up embarrassment, but which simultaneously draws attention to her pretty hands — is doubly flattering.[20] Rather than remain in her rightful position of invisible editor, Éveline interrupts Balzac's prose with what appears to be an unnecessary and even self-gratifying glimpse of herself.

Pommier's analysis somewhat glosses over the possibility that this may not necessarily be about self-admiration or self-aggrandizement, however, but about conforming to normative gender roles. When we remember that Madame Hanska had written the initial draft of *Modeste Mignon,* and then immediately destroyed it, thus shying away from any attempt to put herself forward as a literary figure, we can see just how strong the social pressure was not to appear a bluestocking.[21] When, therefore, in the above extract she paints her modest and pretty gesture, she is protecting herself from appearing overly masculinized — entering, as she now is, the masculine world of literature and literary criticism. Her initial acumen now appears couched, in this new version, within a demure and respectable femininity. Furthermore, Balzac's direct comparison of her to a man, Planche, has conspicuously been removed.

Celebrated female authors such as Madame de Lafayette and George Sand notwithstanding, male authors in nineteenth-century France still appeared unable to believe that women were capable of producing art to equal that of men.[22] Flaubert, for instance, who publicly admired George Sand, privately dismissed her writing as disgustingly feminine: 'Dans G[eorge] Sand, on sent les fleurs blanches; cela suinte, et l'idée coule entre les mots comme entre des cuisses sans muscles' [G[eorge] Sand's writing smells of white flowers; it seeps, oozes, and the ideas flow between the words, like between thighs without muscle].[23] In Balzac's own fictional world, even his most celebrated fictional female author, Camille Maupin, ends her days in a convent, regretting that she had not bowed down to a more conventional lifestyle.[24] Éveline, it would appear, was determined not to attract similar judgements.

Her addition has a further resonance when reappraised within the wider context of the letter into which it was inserted, and in which Balzac commented on her critical flair and writing style. Significantly, in this same letter, Balzac gave her explicit recommendations on how she should write to him, and emphatically criticized her habit of writing lengthy comments in praise of his works — sounding rather like an exasperated grammar teacher, who repeats instructions to his pupil for the umpteenth time:

> *Cara*, [...] Aussi, vous suppliai-je, une fois pour toutes, de supprimer les longs éloges, dites-moi sur trois tons, c'est bien, c'est beau, c'est magnifique, vous aurez là un positif, un comparatif et un superlatif qui sont si grandioses chacun en leur genre que je rougis de les offrir à votre encensoir; mais ils sont encore si loin des gracieusetés louangeuses que vous m'adressez parfois qu'ils sont modestes, ce qui paraîtrait bien singulier à un tiers.[25]

> [*Cara*, [...] Also, I must beg you once and for all to do away with the lengthy praise, tell me using one of these three registers: it is good, it is beautiful, it is magnificent, there you have one positive comment, one comparative and one superlative, each of which is so grandiose in its own way that the very thought of presenting them to your censer makes me blush; but they are still so far away from your laudative graciousnesses that they are in fact modest, which would seem quite odd to a third party.]

If we look at this comment closely, we see that *Balzac* is the one who described his embarrassed blushes, and who called for the text to express more modesty (even if this is to be done in a way which to some readers might not appear particularly modest). It is striking, therefore, that she should have edited his letter in such a way that its reference to her should echo this earlier plea for modesty and recall Balzac's imagery of embarrassment. Whether this was an entirely unintentional coincidence, or whether perhaps Éveline was — albeit subconsciously — employing Balzac's suggestion, we can never know. However, this re-examination of the text should perhaps put us on our guard, as regards our attitude to Éveline's corrections of the published letters. Contrary to Jean Pommier's suggestion, her intention was not to shower herself with praise; rather, her corrections were a well-intentioned (if clumsy) attempt to follow her teacher's instructions whilst also protecting herself.[26] In this same letter, Balzac did in a way give her carte blanche to censure his texts, saying 'j'ai dans votre jugement littéraire une confiance aveugle' [I have a blind confidence in your literary judgment].[27] Requesting her detailed critique of *La*

Vieille Fille, Balzac urged her not to hold back: 'Soyez sans pitié, ni indulgence. Allez-y hardiment' [Be without pity, or indulgence. Go boldly forth].[28] We may wonder whether Balzac's invitation to give her criticism 'boldly', as opposed to demurely, is one which she feels cannot stand up to the sexist assumptions of the wider world, yet which, in her own way, she tries to respect.

Since Balzac and Madame Hanska were perpetually involved in a circle of mutual appraisal and critique (the twenty-seven-year-old Madame Hanska writing to Balzac to tell him what she thought of his novels, and he frequently appraising her letters and her style), and since all letters are inevitably written with their critical recipient in mind, we cannot always tell whose voice is really coming through in a letter. When Balzac writes of 'gracieusetés louangeuses', for example, this overly pompous expression is almost certainly borrowed from his beloved collection of Madame Hanska's peculiar turns of phrase, and is employed here with the intention of poking fun at her; thus the example of the 'gracieusetés' is an instance in which the discerning reader of the correspondence can clearly see the words of Madame Hanska coming through Balzac's text.[29] In the letters that have survived from Éveline to Balzac, then, we cannot be entirely sure which elements derive from her own creative imagination and which are echoes, continuations, or fulfilments of that of Balzac. For this reason, it would be helpful to study the Champfleury letters in some depth in order to come to a detailed understanding of Éveline's writing styles and methods of textual creation.

Following the death of Madame Hanska/Madame de Balzac in 1882, the house in the rue Fortunée was ransacked by creditors; Balzac's papers, which would have fetched good money in a well-organized auction, were thrown into the street. Charles de Spoelberch de Lovenjoul, a Belgian scholar and collector, arrived to hunt for any scraps of Balzac's letters in the *quartier*, saving many of the precious papers from becoming household rubbish. According to later accounts of this very special treasure-hunt (accounts which, as Roger Pierrot suggests, contained a certain amount of fabulation), some of the letters were rescued just in time, Lovenjoul spotting a page just as a vendor was about to use it to wrap up produce.[30] That the letters should have ended up as the property of a collector is one of the many ironies of this correspondence; yet it is also what saved them from destruction, and what led to their publication. It was thanks to Lovenjoul, who first undertook the task of methodically organizing, deciphering, and transcribing Balzac's letters, that the letters were carefully edited and published.[31] Pierrot's research on Balzac and work on the publication of his *Correspondance* brought to light a number of omissions and mistakes in the *Lettres à l'Étrangère*, rectified in the 1990 edition *Lettres à Madame Hanska*.[32]

Roland Barthes has written that all paper (and consequently all writing) is one day destined to become rubbish, no matter what it originally cost for it to be produced.[33] The fact that Balzac's letters survive, having — for now at least — escaped such a fate, and that they can today be read and searched in digital form, is thus a testament not just to the power of his creative imagination but to the empathetic and literary imaginations of Lovenjoul and subsequent scholars, who, like Balzac, understood that through collecting, reading, rereading, and recombining, new stories, new ideas, and new layers of meaning can emerge.

Notes to the Afterword

1. See *LMH*, I, LXXXV.
2. See Robb, p. 405.
3. *LMH*, I, 578 (29 April 1842).
4. Baron, *Hiéroglyphes*, p. 129.
5. *LMH*, I, 7–8 (May 1832).
6. *LMH*, I, 578 (29 April 1842).
7. These letters are published under the name Éveline de Balzac, *Lettres inédites a Champfleury (1851–1854)*, ed. by Lorin A. Uffenbeck and Elizabeth Fudakowska (Paris: Champion; Geneva: Slatkine, 1989). To date, no critical study has been made of the relationship between these letters and Balzac's correspondence with Madame Hanska.
8. Ibid., p. 62.
9. Ibid., p. 31.
10. Ibid., p. 48.
11. See *LMH*, I, 13–16 (7 November 1832), *LMH*, I, 19–20 (8 January 1833), & *LMH*, II, 60 (31 August 1845).
12. See for example *Lettres inédites à Champfleury*, pp. 46 & 110.
13. Martine Reid, *Flaubert correspondant* (Paris: SEDES, 1995), p. 5.
14. One critic has amusingly described this as a 'sérieux toilettage' [serious grooming] (the word 'toilettage' brings to mind 'dog-grooming'). See Brigitte Diaz, *Stendhal en sa correspondance*, p. 22. See also Roger Pierrot, 'Histoire de la publication', *LMH*, I, VII-XXIII (p. VIII).
15. Irene Cornwell, 'The *Correspondance* of Honoré de Balzac: Its Significance and its Unreliability', *PMLA*, 44.4 (December 1929), 1159–78, p. 1167. See also n. 37 on the same page.
16. See *LMH*, I, 376 (10 May 1847), n. 1
17. *LMH*, I, 376 & 375 (10 May 1847).
18. *LMH*, I, 375 (10 May 1837). Jean Baptiste Gustave Planche was a contemporary of Balzac and a French art and literature critic.
19. Honoré de Balzac, *Correspondance*, 2 vols (Paris: Calmann-Lévy, 1876), I, 418–19 (my emphasis). This quotation is discussed by Roger Pierrot, *LMH*, I, 376 (10 May 1847), n. 1.
20. See Jean Pommier, 'Ève de Balzac, sa fille, son amant', *L'Année balzacienne* (1966), 245–85 (p. 246).
21. Balzac reinforced this; for although he initially praised her idea and requested that she write it again, he soon claimed her story as his own, and wrote it himself. See *LMH*, I, 832 (21 March 1844).
22. On nineteenth-century preconceptions of women as critics or intellectuals, see Kimberly Van Esveld Adams, 'Women and Literary Criticism', in *The Cambridge History of Literary Criticism Volume 6: The Nineteenth Century*, ed. M. A. R. Habib, (Cambridge: Cambridge University Press, 2013), pp. 72–94.
23. Flaubert, *Correspondance*, in *Oeuvres completes*, ed. by Bardèche, XII, 250 (16 November 1852). He also complained that 'La littérature contemporaine est noyée [dans les règles de femme]' [Contemporary literature is drenched [in women's periods]] (*Correspondance*, XII, 457, 15 January 1854). This view of Sand changed as he got older. See also Lewis, *Germaine de Staël, George Sand, and the Victorian Woman Artist*.
24. See Gretchen R. Besser, *Balzac's Concept of Genius: The Theme of Superiority in The Comédie humaine* (Geneva: Droz, 1969), pp. 241–42.
25. *LMH*, I, 375 (10 May 1847).
26. Jean Pommier uses the fortuitous phrase 's'encenser soi-même' (in French, 'encenser' is a word play on the notion of burning incense in honour of someone, which has come to mean 'to praise'). Pommier, p. 246.
27. *LMH*, I, 375 (10 May 1847).
28. Ibid.
29. Compare also with instances where Balzac makes fun of her expression 'mauvaisetiés' [badnesses]: *LMH*, I, 46 (8 August 1833); *LMH*, I, 147 (11 March 1834); *LMH*, II, 360 (2 October 1846); and *LMH*, II, 299 (12 August 1846).

30. Roger Pierrot clarifies and expands on existing accounts of the hunt for Balzac's letters, and subsequently the story of their publication following the work of Lovenjoul, in *LMH*, I, IX–XVII.
31. See Pierrot, *LMH*, I, XVIII.
32. Pierrot, *LMH*, I, XIX.
33. 'Le papier écrit a désormais vocation de déchet, de rebut, d'ordure (bien qu'il ait coûté fort cher à son origine)' [All paper that has been written on has the vocation of becoming a piece of rubbish, even if it had had a very high cost at the start], Roland Barthes, *Le Plaisir du texte/Variations sur l'écriture* (Paris: Seuil, 2000), p. 74.

SELECT BIBLIOGRAPHY

❖

Primary Sources: Works by Balzac

BALZAC, HONORÉ DE, *La Comédie humaine*, ed. by Pierre-Georges Castex, 12 vols (Paris: Gallimard, Bibliothèque de la Pléiade, 1976–81)
——*Correspondance*, 2 vols (Paris: Calmann-Lévy, 1876)
——*Correspondance*, ed. by Roger Pierrot and Hervé Yon, 2 vols (Paris: Gallimard, 2006–11)
——*Lettres à Madame Hanska*, ed. by Roger Pierrot, 2 vols (Paris: Laffont, Bouquins, 1990)
——*Pensées, sujets, fragments*, ed. by Jacques Crépet (Paris: Blaizot, 1910)
——*Premiers romans*, ed. by André Lorant, 2 vols (Paris: Laffont, Bouquins, 1999)

Primary Sources: Other Works

BALZAC, ÉVELINE DE, *Lettres inédites a Champfleury (1851–1854)*, ed. by Lorin A. Uffenbeck and Elizabeth Fudakowska (Paris: Champion; Geneva: Slatkine, 1989)
ELIOT, T.S., *Selected Essays* (London: Faber, 1972)
FLAUBERT, GUSTAVE, *Madame Bovary*, ed. by Adolphe Gondry (Paris: Librairie Gruend, 1857)
——*Œuvres complètes*, ed. by Maurice Bardèche, 16 vols (Paris: Club de l'Honnête Homme, 1971)
GAUTIER, THÉOPHILE, 'Affinités secrètes', in *Émaux et camées* (Paris: Les Maîtres du livre, 1913)
——*Mademoiselle de Maupin* (1835)
LACLOS, PIERRE CHODERLOS DE, *Les Liaisons dangereuses* (Paris: Flammarion, 1981)
OVID, *Metamorphoses,* ed. by Madeleine Forey, trans. by Arthur Golding (London: Penguin, 2002)
SARTRE, JEAN-PAUL, *L'Être et le Néant* (Paris: Gallimard, 1943)
STERNE, LAURENCE, *The Life and Opinions of Tristram Shandy, Gentleman*, ed. by Melvyn New and Joan New, 3 vols (Gainesville: University Presses of Florida, 1984)

Secondary Sources

AMOSSY, RUTH, 'La Lettre d'amour du réel au fictionnel', in *La Lettre entre réel et fiction*, ed. by Jürgen Siess (Paris: SEDES, 1998), pp. 73–96
BARBÉRIS, PIERRE, *Aux sources de Balzac: les romans de jeunesse* (Paris: Bibliophiles de l'Originale, 1965)
——*Balzac et le mal du siècle: contribution à une physiologie du monde moderne*, 2 vols (Paris: Gallimard, 1970)
——'Les Mythes de *La Dernière Fée*', *L'Année balzacienne* (1964), 139–80
BARON, ANNE-MARIE, *Balzac et la bible: une herméneutique du romanesque* (Paris: Honoré Champion, 2007)
——*Balzac occulte: alchimie, magnétisme, sociétés secrètes* (Lausanne: L'Age d'Homme, 2012)
——*Balzac ou l'auguste mensonge* (Paris: Nathan, 1998)

——*Balzac ou les hiéroglyphes de l'imaginaire* (Paris: Honoré Champion, 2002)

——'Fantasmes et sublimation dans *Le médecin de campagne*', *L'Année balzacienne* (2003), 77–90

——*Le Fils prodige: l'inconscient de La Comédie humaine* (Paris: Nathan, 1993)

——'L'Intertexte biblique d'*Illusions perdues*', in *'Illusions perdues': colloque de la Sorbonne*, ed. by José-Luis Diaz and André Guyaux, 2nd edn (Paris: Presses de l'Université Paris-Sorbonne, 2004), pp. 11–24

BARTHES, ROLAND, *Le Bruissement de la langue* (Paris: Seuil, 1984)

——*Fragments d'un discours amoureux* (Paris: Seuil, 1977)

——*Le Plaisir du texte / Variations sur l'écriture* (Paris: Seuil, 2000)

——*S/Z* (Paris: Seuil, 1970)

BEIZER, JANET, 'F/V: notes sur *Le Lys dans la vallée*', in *L'Érotique balzacienne*, ed. by Lucienne Frappier-Mazur and Jean-Marie Roulin (Paris: SEDES, 2001), pp. 11–22

BELLOS, DAVID, 'Balzac and Goethe's Bettina', in *Literary Communication and Reception*, Innsbrucker Beiträge zur Kulturwissenschaft, Sonderheft 46 (Innsbruck: AMCE, 1980), pp. 359–64

BESSER, GRETCHEN, *Balzac's Concept of Genius: The Theme of Superiority in The Comédie humaine* (Geneva: Droz, 1969)

BIELECKI, EMMA, *The Collector in Nineteenth-Century Literature: Representation, Identity, Knowledge* (Bern: Peter Lang, 2012)

BIJAOUI-BARON, ANNE-MARIE, 'Henry de Balzac', *L'Année balzacienne* (1979), 211–19

BOUTERON, MARCEL, *Études balzaciennes* (Paris: Jouve, 1954)

——*La Véritable Image de Madame Hanska* (Paris: Lapina, 1929)

BUI, VÉRONIQUE, *La Femme, la faute et l'écrivain: la mort féminine dans l'œuvre de Balzac* (Paris: Champion, 2003)

BUTLER, JUDITH, *Excitable Speech: A Politics of the Performative* (New York & London: Routledge, 1997)

CALINESCU, MATEI, *Rereading* (New Haven, CT, & London: Yale University Press, 1993)

CAVE, TERENCE, *Mignon's Afterlives: Crossing Cultures from Goethe to the Twenty-First Century* (Oxford: Oxford University Press, 2011)

CORNWELL, IRENE, 'The *Correspondance* of Honoré de Balzac: Its Significance and its Unreliability', *PMLA*, 44.4 (December 1929), 1159–78

DARGAN, JOAN, *Balzac and the Drama of Perspective: The Narrator in Selected Works of 'La Comédie humaine'* (Lexington, KY: French Forum, 1985)

DÉGA, JEAN-LOUIS, *La Vie prodigieuse de Bernard-François Balssa: aux sources historiques de 'La Comédie humaine'* (Rodez: Subervie, 1998)

DELAYE, JACQUES, *Madame Honoré de Balzac* (Paris: Perrin, 1989)

DERRIDA, JACQUES, *On the Name*, ed. by Thomas Dutoit, trans. by David Wood and others (Stanford, CA: Stanford University Press, 1995)

DIAZ, BRIGITTE, *L'Épistolaire ou la pensée nomade: formes et fonctions de la correspondance dans quelques parcours d'écrivains au XIXe siècle* (Paris: PUF, 2002)

——*Stendhal en sa correspondence, ou 'L'Histoire d'un esprit'* (Paris: Champion, 2003)

DIAZ, JOSÉ-LUIS, 'A quoi servent les correspondances: l'exemple de Balzac', in *Pour Balzac et pour les livres: hommage à Roger Pierrot*, ed. by Thierry Bodin (Paris, Klincksieck, 1999), pp. 31–40

——'Créer peut-être à deux', *L'Année balzacienne* (2010), 39–58

——*Devenir Balzac: l'invention de l'écrivain par lui-même* (Saint-Cyr-sur-Loire: Christian Pirot, 2007)

DIDI-HUBERMAN, GEORGES, *La Peinture incarnée* (Paris: Minuit, 1985)

DOBSON, TIMOTHY, 'Aspects of the Mother and Child Relationship in Selected Novels of Honoré de Balzac and George Sand' (unpublished doctoral thesis, University of Manchester, 1990)

DUFOUR-KOWALSKI, EMMANUEL, *Balzac et madame Hanska: réminiscences d'un roman d'amour* (Paris: Panthéon, 1994)

FALCONER, RACHEL, and ANDREW OLIVER, eds., *Re-Reading/La Relecture: Essays in Honour of Graham Falconer* (Newcastle upon Tyne: Cambridge Scholars, 2012)

FARRANT, TIM, 'Balzac: du pittoresque au pictural', *L'Année balzacienne* (2004), 113–35

——*Balzac's Shorter Fictions: Genesis and Genre* (Oxford: Oxford University Press, 2002)

——'Burying the Past: De-reading *Dominique*', in *Re-Reading/La Relecture: Essays in Honour of Graham Falconer*, ed. by Rachel Falconer and Andrew Oliver (Newcastle upon Tyne: Cambridge Scholars, 2012), pp. 49–66

FORTASSIER, ROSE, 'Du bon usage par le romancier Balzac des souffrances du jeune Honoré', *Imaginaire & Inconscient* 4 (2003), 39–52

FRAPPIER-MAZUR, LUCIENNE, and JEAN-MARIE ROULIN, EDS, *L'Érotique balzacienne* (Paris: SEDES, 2001)

FREUD, SIGMUND, 'Beyond the Pleasure Principle', in *The Standard Edition of the Complete Psychological Works*, ed. and trans. by James Strachey, 24 vols (London: Hogarth Press, 1953–74), XVIII (1961), pp. 7–64

FRØLICH, JULIETTE, 'L'Ange au pays des neiges: *Séraphîta*', *L'Année balzacienne* (1992), 319–31

——'Balzac, l'objet et les archives romantiques de la création', *L'Année balzacienne* (2000), 145–57

——*Des hommes, des femmes et des choses: langages de l'objet de Balzac à Proust* (Saint-Denis: Presses Universitaires de Vincennes, 1997)

GOETZ, ADRIEN, ' "De si vives compensations à la faillite de la gloire": les collectionneurs au centre de *La Comédie humaine*', in *Balzac et la peinture* (Tours: Musée des Beaux-Arts de Tours/Farrago, 1999), pp. 187–92

GREENE, JOHN PATRICK, 'Balzac's Most Helpless Heroine: The Art Collection in *Le Cousin Pons*', *The French Review*, 69 (October 1995), 13–23

GRIVEL, CHARLES, 'Balzac, *La Comédie humaine:* Notice pour *Séraphîta*', <http://www.vi.paris.fr/commun/v2asp/musees/balzac/furne/notices/seraphita.htm> [accessed 11 November 2012]

GUBAR, SUSAN, '*The Blank Page* and the Issues of Female Creativity', *Critical Inquiry*, 8 (1981), 243–63

GUICHARDET, JEANNINE, *Balzac mosaïque* (Clermont-Ferrand: Presses Universitaires Blaise Pascal, 2007)

——'Honorine ou la fleur de son secret', in *Jardins et intimité dans la littérature européenne (1750–1920): actes du colloque du Centre de recherches révolutionnaires et romantiques, Université Blaise-Pascal, Clermont-Ferrand, 22–24 mars 2006*, ed. by Simone Bernard-Griffiths and others (Clermont-Ferrand: Presses Universitaires Blaise-Pascal, 2008), pp. 185–95

——'Penser/voir avec Balzac: le Paris d'hier et d'aujourd'hui', in *Penser avec Balzac*, ed. by José-Luis Diaz and Isabelle Tournier (Saint-Cyr-sur-Loire: Christian-Pirot, 2003), pp. 83–94

GUYON, BERNARD, *La Création littéraire chez Balzac: la genèse du Médecin de campagne*, 2nd edn (Paris: Colin, 1969)

HEATHCOTE, OWEN, '(Auto-)portrait d'un auteur en courtisane: le travail du sexe et le sexe du travail dans les Lettres à Mme Hanska' in *Paratextes balzaciens: 'La Comédie humaine' en ses marges'*, ed. by Roland Le Huenen and Andrew Oliver (Toronto: Centre d'études du XIX siècle Joseph Sable, 2007), pp. 179–90

——'Balzac Between Work and Play: *Les Comédiens sans le savoir*', *Nottingham French Studies*, 51 (2012), 136–46

——'Spectres de Balzac? Personnage(s) reparaissant(s) et textes préexistants dans *Séraphîta*', *Eidôlon*, 52 (1999), 121–34

HUNT, HERBERT J., *Balzac's Comédie humaine* (London: Athlone, 1964)

JARRY, PAUL, *Le Dernier logis de Balzac, rue Fortunée, etc.* (Paris: Kra, 1924)

JOHNSON, BARBARA, 'The Critical Difference: Barthes/BalZac', in *The Critical Difference: Essays in the Contemporary Rhetoric of Reading* (Baltimore, MD, & London: Johns Hopkins University Press, 1980), pp. 3–12

KAUFMANN, VINCENT, *L'Équivoque épistolaire* (Paris: Minuit, 1990)

——*Post Scripts: The Writer's Workshop*, trans. by Deborah Treisman (Cambridge, MA, & London: Harvard University Press, 1994)

KERBAT-ORECCHIONI, CATHERINE, *Les Interactions verbales* (Paris: Collin, 1990)

KIRIU, KAZUO, *Vocabulaire de Balzac*, <http://www.v2asp.paris.fr/commun/v2asp/musees/balzac/kiriu/> [accessed 11 September 2012]

KNIGHT, DIANA, *Balzac and the Model of Painting: Artist Stories in La Comédie humaine* (Oxford: Legenda, 2007)

——'Balzac's Honorine, or, The Rape of the Independent Woman', in *Women, Genre and Circumstance: Essays in Memory of Elizabeth Fallaize*, ed. by Margaret Atack and others (Oxford: Legenda, 2012), pp. 60–73

KORWIN-PIOTROWSKA, SOPHIE, *Balzac et le monde slave: Madame Hanska et l'œuvre balzacienne* (Paris: Librairie Ancienne Honoré Champion, 1933)

KRISTEVA, JULIA, *Le Génie féminin: la vie, la folie, les mots: Hannah Arendt, Melanie Klein, Colette*, 3 vols (Paris: Fayard, 2002)

——*Pouvoirs de l'horreur: essai sur l'abjection* (Paris: Seuil, 1980)

LE HUENEN, ROLAND, and PAUL PERRON, 'Les Lettres à Madame Hanska: métalangage du roman et représentation du romanesque', *Revue des sciences humaines*, 195 (1984), 25–40

LEJEUNE, PHILIPPE, *Les Brouillons de soi* (Paris: Seuil, 1998)

LEWIS, LINDA M., *Germaine de Staël, George Sand, and the Victorian Woman Artist* (Columbia & London: University of Missouri Press, 2003)

LORANT, ANDRÉ, 'Présentation du *Journal Intime* de Madame Hanska', *L'Année balzacienne* (1962), 3–34

LOTTE, FERNAND, 'Le Retour des personnages dans *La Comédie humaine*: avantages et inconvénients du procédé', *L'Année balzacienne* (1961), 227–81

LOVENJOUL, CHARLES DE SPOELBERCH DE, *Études balzaciennes: un roman d'amour* (Paris: Calmann Lévy, 1896)

McCALL SAINT-SAËNS, ANNE, 'De la haine épistolaire ou "La fatale puissance de la lettre"', in *L'Érotique balzacienne*, ed. by Lucienne Frappier-Mazur and Jean-Marie Roulin (Paris: SEDES, 2001), pp. 41–50

MEYER SPACKS, PATRICIA, *On Rereading* (Cambridge, MA, & London: Belknap, 2011)

MOZET, NICOLE, '1848: Après "La Comédie humaine", le théâtre? Les Lettres à Mme Hanska comme paratexte', in *Paratextes balzaciens: 'La Comédie humaine' en ses marges*, ed. by Roland Le Huenen and Andrew Oliver (Toronto: Centre d'études du XIX siècle Joseph Sable, 2007), pp. 169–78

NABOKOV, VLADIMIR, *Lectures on Literature* (London: Harvest, 1980)

OSUGA, SAORI, *Séraphîta et la Bible: sources scripturaires du mysticisme balzacien* (Paris: Champion, 2012)

PEYLET, GÉRARD, 'De la manie à la mélancolie: les souffrances du créateur balzacien dans la correspondance et dans les romans de 1830', *Eidôlon*, 52 (1999), 147–60

——'Les Souffrances du créateur: de la pathologie à la Passion dans les *Lettres à Madame Hanska* de Balzac', *Eidôlon*, 50 (1997), 323–30

PIERROT, ROGER, *Ève de Balzac* (Paris: Stock, 1999)

——*Honoré de Balzac* (Paris: Fayard, 1994)

PITT-RIVERS, FRANÇOISE, *Balzac et l'art* (Paris: Chêne, 1993)

POMMIER, JEAN, 'Ève de Balzac, sa fille, son amant', *L'Année balzacienne* (1966), 245–85

PORTER-TSOMONDO, THORELL, *The Not So Blank 'Blank Page': The Politics of Narrative and the Woman Narrator in the Eighteenth- and Nineteenth-Century English Novel* (New York: Peter Lang, 2007)

PROUST, MARCEL, *Contre Sainte-Beuve*, ed. by Pierre Clarac and Yves Sandre (Paris: Gallimard, 1971)

PUGH, ANTONY, *Balzac's Recurring Characters* (London: Duckworth, 1975)

REID, MARTINE, *Flaubert correspondant* (Paris: SEDES, 1995)

RICŒUR, PAUL, *The Symbolism of Evil*, trans. by Emerson Buchanan (Boston, MA: Beacon Press, 1969)

ROBB, GRAHAM, *Balzac: A Biography* (London: Picador, 1994)

SAHLI, JANET, 'Le Rôle de l'enfance dans *La Comédie humaine*', *L'Année balzacienne*, (1975), 279–88

SAINT BRIS, GONZAGUE, *Je vous aime inconnue: Balzac et Éva Hanska* (Paris: NiL, 1999)

SCHECHNER, RICHARD, *Between Theatre and Anthropology* (Philadelphia: University of Pennsylvania Press, 1985)

——*Essays on Performance Theory, 1970–1976* (New York: Drama Book Specialists, 1977)

——*Performance Studies: An Introduction*, 2nd edn (New York & London: Routledge, 2006)

SCHUEREWEGEN, FRANC, *Balzac contre Balzac: les cartes du lecteur* (Toronto: SEDES/Paratexte, 1990)

SCHWEIGER, AMÉLIE, 'La Lettre d'orient', *Revue des sciences humaines*, 195 (1984), 41–57

SEGAL, NAOMI, 'To Love and Be Loved: Sartre, Anzieu and Theories of the Caress', *Paragraph*, 32 (July 2009), 226–39

SIBONY, DANIEL, *Les Trois Monothéismes: juifs, chrétiens, musulmans entre leurs sources et leurs destins* (Paris: Seuil, 1992)

STAROBINSKI, JEAN, *Portrait de l'artiste en saltimbanque* (Paris: Gallimard, 2004; repr. 2013)

SURVILLE, LAURE, *Balzac, sa vie et ses œuvres d'après sa correspondance* (Paris: Librairie Nouvelle, 1858)

SZYPULA, EWA, 'An Aesthetics of Indirection in Novels and Letters: Balzac's Communication with Évelina Hanska', in *The Ethics of Literary Communication: Genuineness, Directness, Indirectness*, ed. by Roger Sell, Adam Borch and Inna Lindgren (Amsterdam: John Benjamins, 2013), pp. 229–46

VACHON, STÉPHANE, ed., *Balzac: une poétique du roman* (Saint-Denis: Presses Universitaires de Vincennes, 1996)

——*Les Travaux et les jours d'Honoré de Balzac: chronologie de la création balzacienne* (Paris: Presses Universitaires de Vincennes and Montreal, Presses de l'Université de Montréal, 1992)

VAN ESVELD ADAMS, KIMBERLY, 'Women and Literary Criticism', in *The Cambridge History of Literary Criticism Volume 6: The Nineteenth Century*, ed. by M. A. R. Habib (Cambridge: Cambridge University Press, 2013), pp. 72–94

VOGEL, UWE, *Balzac als Briefschreiber: ein Romancier zwischen Realität und Fiktion* (Frankfurt am Main: Haag & Herchen, 1986)

WATSON, JANELL, *Literature and Material Culture from Balzac to Proust* (Cambridge: Cambridge University Press, 1999)

WETTLAUFER, ALEXANDRA, *Pen vs. Paintbrush: Girodet, Balzac and the Myth of Pygmalion in Postrevolutionary France* (New York: Palgrave, 2001)

ZWEIG, STEFAN, *Balzac*, trans. by William and Dorothy Rose, 2nd edn (London: Cassell, 1970)

INDEX

❖